MENSA MIND WORKOUT

THIS IS A CARLTON BOOK

This Edition published by Carlton Books Limited 1999

A CIP catalogue for the book is available from the British Library

ISBN 1 85868 546 X

Editor: Tim Dedopulos
Senior Art Editor: Zoe Maggs
Design: Giles Ellis
Production: Garry Lewis

Printed in Great Britain

MENSA MIND WORKOUT

Josephine Fulton

CARLTON

CONTENTS

AMERICAN MENSA LIMITED

American Mensa Ltd is an organization for people who have one common trait: an IQ in the top 2% of the nation. Over 50,000 current members have found out how smart they are. This leaves room for an additional 4.5 million members in America alone. You may be one of them.

If you enjoy mental exercise, you'll find lots of good "workout programs" in the *Mensa Bulletin*, our national magazine. Voice your opinion in one of the newsletters published by each of our 150 local chapters. Learn from the many books and publications that are available to you as a member.

Are you a "people person," or would you like to meet other people with whom you feel comfortable? Then come to our local meetings, parties, and get-togethers. Participate in our lectures and debates. Attend our regional events and national gatherings. There's something happening on the Mensa calendar almost daily. So, you have lots of opportunities to meet people, exchange ideas, and make interesting new friends. Maybe you're looking for others who share your special interest? Whether yours is as common as crossword puzzles or as esoteric as Egyptology, there's a Mensa Special Interest Group (SIG) for it.

Take the challenge. Find out how smart you really are. Contact American Mensa Ltd today and ask for a free brochure. We enjoy adding new members and ideas to our high-IQ organization.

American Mensa Ltd,
1229 Corporate Drive West,
Arlington, TX 76006-6103.

Or, if you don't live in the USA and you'd like more details, you can contact Mensa International, 15 The Ivories, 628 Northampton Street, London N1 2NY, England, who will be happy to put you in touch with your own national Mensa.

Developing Learning Skills

Does the prospect of learning a foreign language or trying to master the latest piece of equipment at work fill you with apprehension? The first step in overcoming this is to develop confidence in yourself. Learning anything new often seems daunting, but telling yourself that you cannot possibly do it is the guaranteed route to failure.

If you think about the impressive range of skills that you possess, you will realize that it is only your own anxieties that are holding you back. The skills that you use from day to day may seem very ordinary, but in fact they represent a vast amount of knowledge that you have already taken in your stride. Answering the questions below should help to make you more aware of your enormous learning potential.

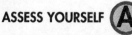

A ASSESS YOURSELF

1. Can you walk? yes

2. Can you talk? yes

3. Can you distinguish between different shapes/sounds/ textures and so on? yes

4. Are you numerate and literate, even at the most elementary level? yes

5. Can you make a cup of coffee? yes

6. Can you cook? yes

7. If not, do you know how to order a takeaway?

n/a

8. Can you go out and buy a loaf of bread?

yes

9. Can you cross the road safely?

yes

10. Do you have a fairly clear idea of your likes and dislikes? yes

11. Can you communicate these to others?

yes

12. Do you have any hobbies? Think about the skills, however basic, that you need for these.

no, yes

13. Do you know any words of a foreign language?

14. Can you drive?

15. If not, are you familiar with other public or private means of getting around?

16. Have you ever taken on any kind of work, either paid or voluntary?

17. Are you familiar with any technological equipment, from telephones and hi-fis to the Internet?

18. Can you change a plug, or know who to contact if you can't?

19. Can you name 10 other countries?

20. Can you name the President of the USA?

These questions should have highlighted the wide range of skills and information that you have acquired since birth – simply surviving from day to day requires a continuous cycle of learning. Now turn to the following tests to give yourself an idea of just how good your learning abilities are.

How Does it Work?

Study the instructions for the various imaginary gadgets listed below. After 10 minutes, cover them up and attempt the multiple-choice questions to discover how much information has registered.

1. The Ho-hum

To operate safely, only remove the protective shield when cutting is in progress. Align the heel at the appropriate foot-size mark and set the gender dial. When all is in place, raise the shield and activate the red button. The blue dial controls the degree of nail trim. Activating the green button switches the Ho-hum off, and automatically lowers the shield, after a 10-second period, to allow for foot removal.

2. The Didgerer

The Didgerer is not suitable for use in very confined spaces. To operate, aim the pointed end towards the animal, ideally within a distance of 12 feet to guarantee accuracy. Click the protruding end in, while still pointing toward the animal to activate the sensory device. Releasing the end at any time results in the catcher being automatically wound in. The Didgerer is effective with both still and moving creatures, with minimal trauma.

3. The Doodar

Switch the Doodar on after ensuring that all 5 batteries are correctly in place. Using the arrow keys, highlight the 6 adjectives characterizing your current mood from the Trait List appearing on screen. Finally, move the cursor to "All" to register your mood and to display a choice of aromatic remedies. After detailing your current location as prompted, a list of outlets supplying the aromatherapy oils is displayed, with details of stock levels. After use, simply switch off.

4. The Whatsitsname

Having produced your chosen culinary mixture, set the white Whatsitsname gauge to the switch that is relevant to the mixture, e.g. cake base, savoury sauce etc. Place the sterilized Whatsitsname into the mixture, and stir for 5 seconds. Remove and wipe to determine the exact amount of thickening agent (provided) required to produce the perfect consistency. Place in the sterilizer before further use in order to clean and reset the device.

5. The Heebie-jeeby

Using the suction pads, attach a Heebie-jeeby centrally on each window after leaving the vehicle during cold weather, particularly at night. Place the rectangular Heebie-jeebies on the front and rear windscreens, and the square Heebie-jeebies on the smaller side windows. To activate, turn the circular switch on each one clockwise until the arrow is level with the orange dot. Remove when using the vehicle, whose windows will be frost-free. When the switch is jammed towards the yellow dot, recharging is necessary.

Questions

1. How many adjectives are used to describe your mood on the Doodar? **a)** 8 **b)** 5 **c)** 6 **d)** 7 **e)** 4

2. What gadget is used in connection with animals?
   a) Whatsitsname **b)** Heeby-jeeby **c)** Ho-hum
   d) Didgerer **e)** Doodar

3. What controls the degree of nail trim on one of the gadgets?
   a) a blue button **b)** a blue switch **c)** a green switch
   d) a blue dial **e)** a green button

4. Where should you not use the Didgerer?
   a) in a car **b)** in a ballroom **c)** in a park
   d) in a department store **e)** on a mountain

5. Which of the following is a named feature of the Ho-hum?
   a) suction pads **b)** protective shield **c)** white gauge
   d) battery-operated mechanism **e)** sensory device

6 What shape should the gadget that sits on the rear windscreen be?

a) circular **b)** triangular **c)** rectangular **d)** square **e)** irregular

7 What is used to reset the Whatsitsname?

a) a cleanser **b)** a dial **c)** a white gauge **d)** a green button **e)** a sterilizer

8 What must be detailed to register a list of outlets on one of the gadgets?

a) your current geographical location **b)** your foot-size **c)** your home address **d)** your current mood **e)** your car

9 How should the switch on the Heeby-jeeby be activated?

a) pressed in **b)** turned clockwise **c)** clicked **d)** pulled out **e)** pushed up

10 Within how many feet should the Didgerer be operated?

a) 6 **b)** 15 **c)** 8 **d)** 10 **e)**12

Finding the Right Words

Study this list of words and accompanying definitions for 5 minutes only – efficient learning is related to speed. Then cover these up, look at the two lists of definitions and words that follow, and match them up. Beware of the red herrings! The test definitions are worded differently from those in the first list, which means that the ability to learn and understand, and not just a good memory, are vital to do well. Of course, if you are already familiar with any of the words, you will have to account for this when scoring.

Lamellibranch: animal of the mollusc class

Eupepsia: good digestion

Afrormosia: African teaklike wood

Riparian: inhabiting or situated on a river bank

Nidifugous: (of birds) leaving their nest soon after being hatched

Imbroglio: confused state of affairs

Nagelfluh: Swiss or Italian conglomerate rock

Guaiacum: South-American tree whose components are medicinal

Now cover up and get matching!

Definitions:

1. Pertaining to a slope by water
2. Hard, yellow-brown plant material
3. Young fledgling active at an early age
4. Soft-bodied animal with a hard shell
5. Perplexing situation
6. Large plant bearing therapeutic properties
7. The satisfactory processing of food in the stomach
8. European coarse-grained mineral matter

Pick out which of these words match the definitions:

- (A) Gualica
- (B) Nagelfluh
- (C) Imbroglio
- (D) Samelibranch
- (E) Afrormosia
- (F) Eupepsicum
- (G) Riparicer
- (H) Imbragsia
- (I) Nidifugous
- (J) Bagelflew
- (K) Riparian
- (L) Eupepsia
- (M) Lamellibranch
- (N) Guaiacum

These kinds of tests give you a good general idea of your ability to learn, and yet they cannot tell the whole story. Learning is a complex process and your capacity to digest, retain and recall information is greatly influenced by the situation you find yourself in, and the way in which information is presented to you.

Early Influences

Our ability and desire to learn stems predominantly from our childhood. Learning to walk and talk is largely a matter of mirroring and repetition, so the degree of encouragement and attention that you receive has a huge influence on your early progress. Anyone with a younger brother or sister will no doubt remember how annoyed they sometimes felt about being constantly copied. Only later in life do we realize just how valuable this learning process is.

From birth onwards, we learn through a continual cycle of habituation – getting used to something – and readjustment. A baby's initial encounter with anything new is often greeted with terror. Only reassurance and closer examination will reveal that the rocking horse, for example, really is harmless.

All of us have a deep-seated desire to question the world around us. As children, "why?" is a key word in our vocabulary. Unfortunately, the path of learning is too often blocked by other people's negative responses – what can any child learn from being told "because it does"? Criticism is equally harmful. If a child is told that his or her handwriting is dreadful, that child may well take this as a direct attack on their personality. This could seriously damage their confidence, and consequently dampen further motivation to learn. What is needed, for children and adults alike, is positive encouragement and ways of teaching that clearly separate someone's personality from the skills they are trying to master. With this approach, our learning skills should flourish, from birth right through to our mature years.

There are other influences from our early years that affect our attitude toward learning in later life. Fond memories of being read to, or helped to read, at bedtime often means that reading is subconsciously linked with pleasure. This could be the start of a lifelong love of reading, which will undoubtedly help to make us more efficient learners.

PUT IT INTO PERSPECTIVE

What is Learning?

The information we take in when we are reading is stored in the many millions of cells that make up the human brain. These cells are connected by a vast network of pathways known as dentritic spines. Acquiring new knowledge doesn't mean that the brain gets too "full" and information is lost in some way – instead, it causes the brain to develop additional pathways. Put simply, the more you learn, the more you are able to learn.

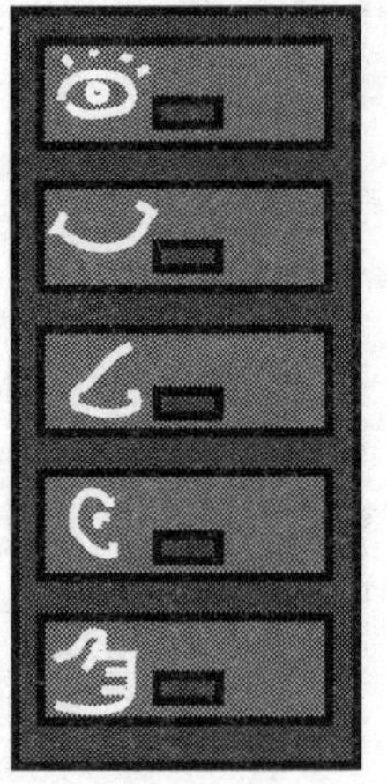

Each of us learns in different ways. For example, ask a friend to observe you discretely at some point in the future when you are in the middle of a discussion. You must be unaware of this, so that you act in a perfectly natural way. How do your mannerisms and facial expressions change when you are asked a question, and when you are listening? What happens to your eyes?

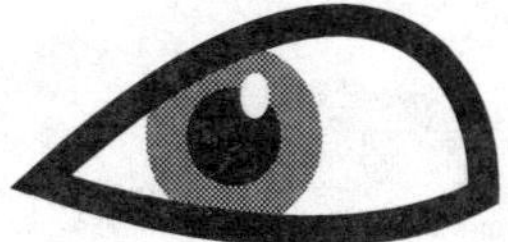

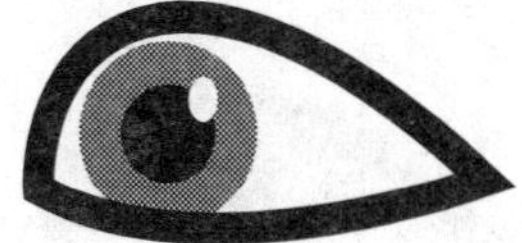

Some people believe that close observation of how your eyes move when you are interacting with others can reveal the way in which you prefer to learn and process information. If your eyes dart upward when you are asked a question or are trying to remember something, you could be someone who responds well to visual images. This is thought to be because you are glancing toward the top of the head which, roughly speaking, is where the eyes are located. This tendency might be emphasized by a preference for using visual language, such as "let's see" and "my view is..." Visual learning can be highly effective because images are often much more appealing and accessible than words. When you pick up a newspaper, are your eyes instantly drawn to the opening paragraph of a story or the photograph that goes with it?

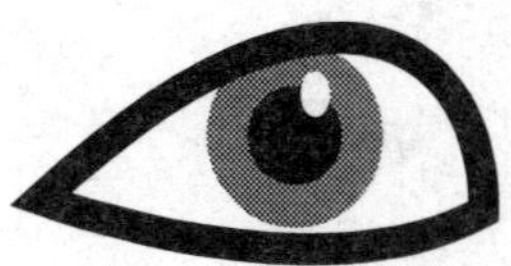

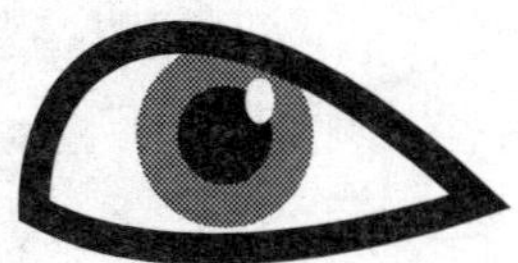

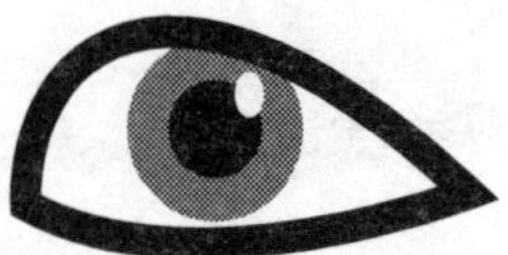

According to this theory, eyes darting to the side, toward the ears, can reflect a reliance on sound and hearing. Again, someone who responds well to sound may use language that reflects this: "I hear you..." "Sounds like a good idea" and so on. Sound is certainly important to all of us as we learn – the tone of a voice, as well as its modulation and volume, can make a huge difference to how we take in spoken information. Stress on one word rather than another could make all the difference to the message we are receiving from the speaker. Also, a narrative delivered with lively enthusiasm and using the full range of the voice is much more memorable than one spoken in flat, inexpressive tones – the ear as well as the mind must be stimulated to maintain your interest and optimize your learning capacity.

The other senses – taste, touch and smell – also play a vital role in our learning processes. Schools and colleges now place great emphasis on active self-discovery, using the full range of the senses, as opposed to relying on passive reading. Recollection of information or past experiences can often be triggered through a familiar smell or taste rather than words.

Think about how you, as an individual, rely on your senses to learn. What sort of language do you use or respond well to? Perhaps you would like to "chew this over" or the answer may be "on the tip of your tongue". Hopefully, you don't "smell a rat". Being aware of the learning potential that your senses offer can not only intensify your powers of understanding, but give your life another fascinating and enjoyable dimension, too.

TEST IT OUT

In the final analysis, you alone control your ability and desire to learn. Advice from others is all very well, but unless you make an effort to use it, no one can help you. The tips on learning technique outlined below are largely a matter of common sense, yet many people completely overlook them. Take the plunge and decide to review your current method of learning now – you might discover that you are missing out on all kinds of learning opportunities.

Tips for Positive Thinking

1. **Your state of mind** dictates your ability to learn and succeed. If you tell yourself that you can't do something, the chances are you won't be able to. Instead of imposing these restrictions on yourself, think positive and focus on what you can do.

2. **Try treating your brain as a sophisticated filing cabinet,** containing positive and negative files. If you have a problem with numbers, for example, try shifting this mentally from a negative to a positive file. You will find that this can alter all kinds of subconscious preconceptions and totally alter the way you view your skills.

3

Always stress what you have got right, rather than what went wrong. This encourages a positive outlook and a heightened desire to know more. Everybody makes mistakes, but realizing how much you have learned in order to get as far as you have can boost your confidence and keep you going through the most difficult of situations.

4

Learn from your mistakes. Dejection is much more likely to set in if your mistakes always prompt feelings of failure rather than providing springboards for further progress. Work through your errors and try to gain something from them – don't give up and start resorting to wild guesses that will teach you nothing.

5

The way in which you deal with the past, present and future is a vital area of learning. Learning is much easier if you try to connect new information with past experience. When trying to remember a date, for instance, associating the numbers with those of a particular birthday or house number may prove invaluable. In this way, fresh information complements your existing store of knowledge rather than becoming a new file in the brain that is inevitably harder to locate.

6

Use visualization techniques to help you take on new information with greater ease. Try imagining yourself standing in the middle of a long road. Your past knowledge stretches away behind you, and the way ahead – your future learning path – is totally uncluttered.

The sky's the limit. Success is not limited – you need to recognize that you can never learn too much. The opportunities are always there, just waiting to be grasped.

No one else can help you if you don't help yourself. If you're confused about something, say so! Coming clean early on could prevent all kinds of complex problems and embarrassment later on.

9

Take notice of what makes other people succeed. Do you have a real problem with complicated calculations, for example, whereas your colleague manages them with ease? Instead of simply feeling resentful, try and find out how they approach the task. Some people believe that if you go even further and imitate some of the mannerisms and attitudes of that person, you can begin to get under their skin and so excel in the same areas. Your life cannot be a constant act, however – use the experience to question where you are going wrong and to get yourself on the right path.

10

Reinforcement is sure to improve your powers of retention. This can mean questioning and participation, reading around a certain subject to add to your understanding, reviewing your knowledge at regular intervals, drawing up effective revision plans, and so on. Revision plans should be viewed as a fundamental part of an effective course of learning. When reading, a continual cycle of skimming, questioning, note-taking and recall testing is guaranteed to produce results to be proud of. The more time you spend planting an idea in your head, the harder it will be to uproot it.

11

Reading and writing are not the only ways to learn and remember. Look and listen carefully to everything around you. Use visual images if you respond well to those – a visual image of a lecturer in action can often trigger information you thought was lost. This does mean, however, that you need to watch and listen carefully to the lecturer in the first place!

12

Be creative. Play around with ideas by creating poems, sketches, and songs around the subject-matter in question. Nurture your creativity. Because it is so valuable in helping you to stay interested in a subject, it may repay you with interest.

13

Experiment with music for the mind. While many prefer to study information in silence, some people say that certain types of music actually help them to learn – which type is up to you to discover. You may well find that it helps your concentration as well as increasing your enjoyment of the learning process.

14

Give yourself a break. If you study from dawn until dusk, your interest will wane, and your learning ability will start to slow down. Try to maintain a balanced lifestyle, and keep your course of learning in perspective. Learn to take regular breaks and vary your environment – try a 5-minute walk around the garden. Constant study may well nourish your conscience, but your mind, like your body, is not programmed for endless exercise, and needs a chance to draw breath every now and again.

15

Establish the learning environment that is best for you. Some people thrive on early morning study, while others cannot even pick up a book until the evening. Experiment a little and discover your best learning environment – the hour, day or place that brings out the best in you. This may also encourage you to feel at ease with the prospect of learning, which is always beneficial.

16

When you can find an interesting or amusing slant to something, you are much more likely to take it in. Making learning stimulating and entertaining helps maximize your motivation and achievement.

17

Feel good about life, your health and learning, and your performance will follow. Look after your body, and your brain will perform much better. You are in the driving seat, and all kinds of learning opportunities are waiting just around the corner. The speed with which you reach them is up to you.

How Does it Work?

Answers

1.c 2.d 3.d 4.a 5.b
6.c 7.e 8.a 9.b 10.e

Your score

6 or less correct: Poor. Don't be discouraged – this is the kind of skill that can easily be improved.

7 or 8 correct: Good. Having a look at a few alternative learning techniques could improve your performance even more.

9 or 10 correct: Excellent. You have highly tuned talents where learning and recall are concerned. You might still benefit from looking at different learning strategies, however.

Finding The Right Words

Answers

1K. 2E. 3I. 4M. 5C. 6N. 7L. 8B.

Your Score.

4 or below: Needs improvement.

5 or 6 correct: Good.

7 or 8 correct: Excellent.

Maximize Your Memory

An efficient memory can add so much to your life, and yet many people simply say things like, "Oh, don't ask me, I can never remember a thing" and do nothing to make matters better. The following tests will help you to identify your position on the memory scale, pinpointing specific areas for self-improvement.

Use the following questionnaire to get a good general impression of how well your memory performs on a day-to-day basis.

Scoring

Circle the number that you consider to be most appropriate: circle 1 if the statement definitely applies to you; 2 if this is the case sometimes, or you aren't quite sure; 3 if this is never the case.

1. When bumping into a long-lost acquaintance in the street, I can rarely remember his or her name.

   1 2 3

2. I tend to forget people's birthdays if I don't have some kind of written reminder.

   1 2 3

3. When reading a book, I can quite easily forget what I've just read in the previous chapter.

   1 2 3

4. Food shopping without a list often means that I end up having to make extra trips to the store.

   1 2 3

5. I have been guilty of forgetting to pass on vital phone messages.

   1 2 3

6. I often rely on other people to remind me to do a particular thing.

   1 2 3

7. It seems to take me ages to master any new words or foreign phrases.

   1 2 3

8. It's unlikely that I would be able to remember a phone number if someone said it to me on the spur of the moment.

   1 2 3

9. After being distracted in mid-conversation, I sometimes find myself asking what I was talking about before I was interrupted.

   1 2 3

10. When it comes to following instructions for a recipe or a complicated gadget, I need to refer to them even after I've cooked the dish or used the gadget several times.

1 2 3

11. I have a tendency to forget either to watch a specific TV programme or to set the VCR for something I wanted to see.

1 2 3

12. I have burned food before now simply because I forgot it was in the oven.

1 2 3

13. Occasionally, I have waited ages for the kettle to boil and then realized that I have forgotten to switch it on.

1 2 3

14. I sometimes over-sleep when I have failed to set the alarm clock.

1 2 3

15. I have been known to turn up at a class or at work, having left an important document at home.

1 2 3

16. When I have stored something valuable in a "safe" place, it sometimes takes me a long time to hunt it out again.

1 2 3

17. If I'm taking some medicine, there will be times when I find myself wondering whether or not I have actually taken it.

1 2 3

18. I have sometimes totally forgotten to make a vital phone call.

1 2 3

19. I have trouble remembering which key is which when I'm carrying quite a few around with me.

1 2 3

20. I rarely remember what I've spent all my money on.

1 2 3

Number Memory

In a world dominated by advanced telecommunications, and the many numerical codes that go with this, a good memory for numbers can make your life a whole lot easier. Test your short-term number memory by reading each of the following lines of digits aloud once, then turning away to write the numbers down in the same order.

5
31
394
7289
31086
618731
1047924
98714389
579489160

Scoring

For each line, see how many digits in a row you manage to remember correctly before making a mistake. When you get to the longer lines of numbers, see what your average score is (a score of 5 equals 5 numbers in a row remembered correctly).

5

3 1

3 9 4

7 2 8 9

3 1 0 8 6

6 1 8 7 3 1

1 0 4 7 9 2 4

9 8 7 1 4 3 8 9

5 7 9 4 8 9 1 6 0

1 7 8 6 9 7 3 8 7 5

Visual Memory

Images can often be stored away in the memory and recalled much more efficiently than numbers or words. This is particularly true if the images are related in some way. Study these objects, all of which have something to do with the head or face, for 1 minute. Now turn the book over and make a list of the objects you can recall.

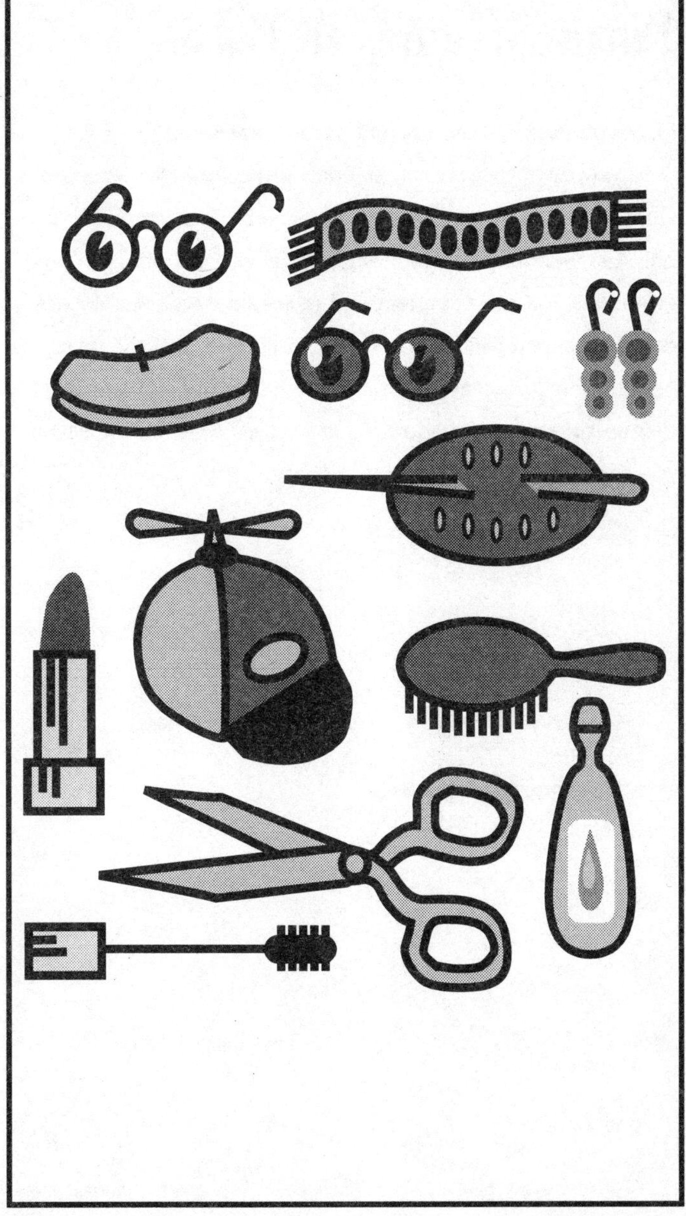

Putting Names to Faces

Have you ever had the uncomfortable experience of bluffing your way through a chance meeting in the street with someone whose identity has completely eluded you? If so, you will know only too well that remembering a visual image is often of little use unless you can put a name to it. See how well you do when trying to remember the names and occupations of the following 12 uniformed people. You have two minutes before covering this box up, turning to the anonymous faces on page 44, and seeing if you can give their identities back to them.

Scoring

Score 2 for each person for whom you gave both the correct name and occupation, 1 if you got either one or the other correct, and 0 if you got neither correct. You will soon discover just how much easier visual images can be to recall than names.

I have a photographic memory, but just occasionally I forget to take off the lens cap

(anon – joke)

When you say "Oh dear, I've completely forgotten" about something, you might think that whatever it is you've forgotten is no longer stored in your memory and is lost forever. This is not the case. An inefficient memory is much more likely to be caused by an inability to recall things, rather than a failure to retain the information in the first place.

To take just a couple of examples, have extremely precise details and images from long ago suddenly burst into your consciousness, although they seemed lost for years? Or has a dream ever unexpectedly come to mind? A vast mass of information is locked away in your memory – all you have to do is find the key.

Where does memory come from?

It seems that memory is not exclusively connected with one particular part of the brain. Because of the countless links between the huge numbers of brain cells, memory processes are constantly taking place all over this remarkable organ. More specific types of memory are, however, thought to spring from specific regions of the brain. An area called the limbic system, for example, is thought to have strong links with the way in which we record and recall general impressions. This is also the region that controls raw emotion, sex drive and appetite. Short-term memory, which lasts up to about 30 seconds, appears to be controlled by the temporal lobes on each side of the brain, while the parietal lobes behind the ears seem to be responsible for retaining knowledge of simple tasks. Visual memory occurs in the occipital lobes at the rear of the brain.

What this means is that serious damage to any of these regions of the brain can have severe consequences for the memory. In one case, a man whose temporal lobes had been badly damaged by an accident was left unable to recall the details of any recent events. Keeping up with the plot of a movie or simply knowing where he had been just a few hours previously became impossible tasks. So next time you complain about how poor your memory is, think again!

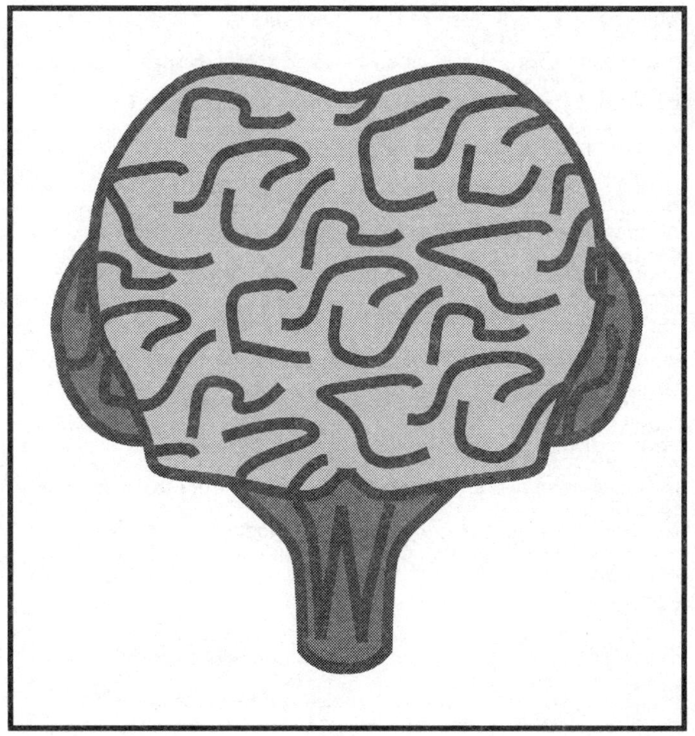

A question of age

Age is directly related to memory skills, so there is little point in comparing the memory of a nine- and a ninety-year-old. For example, as young children, our frontal lobes, which are linked to the way we use language, are not yet fully developed. This means that a child's ability to distinguish between fact and fiction and to remember things accurately is also under-developed. How many times must this have been at the root of arguments between

PUT IT IN PERSPECTIVE

siblings, each convinced of their own version of a family saga? Just talking about things often helps to clear up some of these kinds of discrepancies, because verbal stimulation can trigger all kinds of memories.

At the other end of the scale, memory is said to deteriorate with age. But if you consider how many more memories seventy-year-olds have to contend with compared to their young grandchildren, it's hardly surprising that a few fall by the wayside! This may well be the result of a "last-in, first-out" principle: with new information constantly overlapping old, early memories are frequently the more memorable. It's easy enough to recall the last meal you ate, but could you remember what you had for lunch exactly a month ago today?

There is encouraging evidence that older people today have far more efficient memories than their counterparts in previous generations. The sheer potential of the memory has been hugely underestimated in the past – now each year brings new scientific insights into the workings of the brain and memory, and there seems to be no limit to what can be achieved.

Remembering ... and forgetting

Apart from age, there are many other factors that affect memory – not least of which is information overload. The continual barrage of new information that many of us face every day will inevitably affect the amount of knowledge to which we have instant access. Learning something fresh is never easy when your head is full of all kinds of other information. What is needed to overcome this problem is an organized, firmly focused mind.

Remembering is not the sole function of an efficient memory – much of what we "forget" also plays a vital role in our lives. If we were able to recall every single piece of trivia, from the exact dialogue of every conversation we have ever had to the precise ingredients of every meal we have eaten, then locating important bits of information would be a superhuman task. The extremely selective nature of the memory not only smooths our path in life, but it also interprets the past in a manner that fits in with our desires. This "editing" effect has both good and bad consequences. On one hand, it means that unpleasant memories can be wiped, which may often be a good thing. On the other hand, it means that events can be grossly distorted. This is why it is essential to talk about shared memories with other people, in order to stay as objective as possible.

Giving yourself a prompt

Just as conversation can cause memories to come flooding back, so can specific circumstances or events, whether these are related to sight, smell or sound. Forgotten details can often be unlocked by making a return visit to a relevant environment. Obviously, if you want to jolt memories of a trip around the world, this method might not be feasible, but if you left your keys somewhere while out shopping, retracing your steps may prove invaluable.

As we've already mentioned in the learning chapter, it may be that the eyes play an important role in revealing how we recall events. Some research suggests that people's eyes immediately dart upward, downward, to the left or to the right when asked to recall matters that they connect strongly with their hearing, sight or touch. Darting in one particular direction could mean that the memories in question relate to a specific sense – looking sideways, towards the ears, for example, may indicate the auditory sense. Like the different ways of learning that we've already looked at, an efficient memory often stems from making full use of all of the senses.

The three major ways of learning and remembering are:

REPETITION | ASSOCIATION | VISUALIZATION

Repeating Yourself Yourself Yourself

Simple repetition is not always enough for really effective learning and recollection, and repeating things over and over is not calculated to fill most people with enthusiasm. Repetition tends to produce effective recall only where simpler tasks are concerned. For more complex ones, properly organized memorizing is needed. Various techniques can be used. For example, the ability to recall written information is helped greatly by note-taking and by regular reviews – after half an hour, a day, a month.

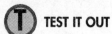

The Art of Association

When it comes to everyday life, and the need to remember a friend's phone number or what to buy at the supermarket, it's time to turn to a more approachable method – mnemonics. Mnemonics are simple, effective tricks to improve your memory, while stimulating your creativity at the same time. Repeating a phone number in your head because you don't have a pen with you could serve you well until you get home and write it down, but what are your chances of recalling the same number a week or month later without any other aid? Instead, try the following mnemonic method. Form a sentence by picking a word to represent each digit. The word should have the same number of letters as the digit it represents. For example:

The number **346443** could be remembered as
"all (3 letters) good (4) things (6) take (4) time (4) too (3)."

Try remembering the reference number **B437 FEM**, a mix of numbers and letters, with:
"Bedraggled (B) ants (4) ate (3) eagerly (7) for (F) eight (E) minutes (M)."

This method of association is easy to master – the more you do it, the easier it becomes. You will also find it an entertaining way of expanding your creative skills.

Using your visualizing skills

Images are also excellent memory aids. A written diary could become a thing of the past if more people developed the various tried and tested visual mnemonic techniques. Try remembering specific objects or events by placing them within a familiar visual context. For example, you might need to remember to find out about booking a trip abroad. Now imagine a walk through a very familiar place – your home or the local park, for example. As you go, insert images of relevant items – a wallet might remind you to work out how much foreign currency you need for your trip.

This method is an excellent one for remembering a list of objects or a sequence of events – from a shopping list to the step-by-step procedure for converting one program to another on your computer. You could try making the first thing that you pass on your route the most important item or event. Or perhaps the order of the images might mirror the chronological order of the events you are trying to memorize. In this way, the schedule for your week ahead might be committed to memory by a mental walk around your garden. Visualize a computer sinking beneath the waters of your pond (finish that vital report); a casket overflowing with coins under the oak tree (chase up unpaid invoices); a huge conductor's baton in the vegetable patch with tomato plants growing up it (a concert outing one evening), and so on...

The surroundings should remain unchanged, only the images you have inserted in order to remind you of something must be new. Ideally, the same scene with the same route should be used for every list you ever want to keep in your mind – with frequent use, remembering lists will become automatic.

If you make the added items and their position within your scenario obscure, out of place or amusing, they will linger in your memory much longer. The image of a giant fish, wearing sunglasses and relaxing happily in your bath, would make you much more likely to remember to buy that fish tank!

Playing the system

You can begin to see just how effective systematic memory methods can be. Look at the letter triangle below. Read it through as if it were normal text, then cover it up and try to reproduce it yourself.

S
T N
A H P
E L E Y
T N I A D

Rather than storing information in countless single pieces, and laboriously fighting through them all in search of what you need, storing chunks of information enables quicker, more efficient access. Remembering two words is far easier than recalling 15 separate and seemingly random letters. Just as documents can be rapidly retrieved from a filing cabinet divided into a logical sequence of ordered sections, so information be recalled more easily from a well-structured memory. Of course one person will use a different filing system to another – test yourself to discover what works best for you.

Recalling written material

Being able to retain and recall text is a vital skill for school, college, work and hobbies. Yet most people fail to organize the way in which they read and run the risk of losing up to 80% of the information after just 24 hours. So resolve to follow the BARCS system next time you want to be able to recall something you are reading:

Breaks:

Have frequent short breaks between intensive periods of study, preferably after 45 minutes to an hour. Try to break for about 15 mins if you can, but any break is better than none. View this as a necessity, not an indulgence.

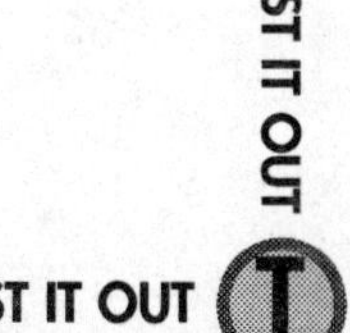

TEST IT OUT

Activity:

The memory performs much more efficiently if you approach reading actively. Take notes, read aloud, walk around the garden with the text – anything to help focus your attention.

Reviews:

Review your previous learning session after each break – just take a couple of minutes to note down what you can remember.

Comparisons:

Compare your notes with the original text. Any errors or omissions will be drilled further into your memory.

Strengthen:

Spend a few minutes reinforcing the summarized material – a day later, a week later and a month later. You should find that much of this information will stay at your fingertips for a long time.

Your reading skills are closely intertwined with your powers of retention. If you learn to retain things more efficiently, you will find yourself reading faster, and focusing your attention more intensely. And time may be of the essence – for a student, less time spent reading means more time for valuable revision. Reading skills are examined in more depth later on (see pages 42–56).

Pay Attention, But Enjoy Yourself Too

Failure to remember things cannot simply be attributed to a poor memory. Recollection may be impossible because the information simply wasn't absorbed and retained in the first place. Fundamental to an efficient memory is the ability to pay attention – if your mind wanders off to distant places while you are being told how to use a new computer, how can you even expect to remember how to turn the machine on?

Learn to concentrate on important details. When meeting new business clients, repeat their names over and over silently to yourself, making a mental note of any helpful associations. You might meet a Ms Redland, and remember her name because she has quite a reddish, ruddy complexion. Distinctive characteristics serve as great memory aids – as ever, the sillier, the better!

Improving your memory can be fun, and you can achieve astonishingly impressive results very quickly. Party games demanding the rapid memorizing of a tray of objects is quite literally child's play – making up a story that links the apparently unconnected items lodges them firmly in the memory.

TEST IT OUT

Some people can "magically" memorize the exact order of an entire pack of playing cards. The method, however, is simple: give the cards identities that you can then link up in the correct sequence. Perhaps you might like to remember each card as a member of a couple of sports teams, for example. Again, it's simply a matter of bundling together disparate images to form a collective group.

Rhymes can also prove to be highly entertaining memory-joggers. Just think of the children's rhymes that you sang years ago, yet can still remember. You could well find that your rhyming experiments render written lists unnecessary. Either compose your own little ditties, full of relevant references, or use a predetermined list of significant words. For this, try assigning a word to each letter of your name. If your name was Jane, this might be jumper for J, apple for A, and so on. Now try to connect each item on the list to each of these words in some way and create your rhyme. You can have a lot of fun making up really bizarre rhymes, but you will need to imprint jumper, apple etc on your memory – remember to remember!

The Role of Your Subconscious

Your subconscious plays a huge role in influencing what you can and cannot remember. Anything your mind connects with fear and unease is guaranteed to impair performance – it's highly likely that at least once in your life you have emerged from a long-dreaded examination of some sort feeling really stupid because you forgot a basic fact or theory. Try to spend time relaxing and preparing yourself mentally for any stressful situations that require a healthily functioning memory. Pinpointing the cause of your fear should enable you to tackle it positively and leave your memory free of unnecessary hindrances. Adequate preparation will help to ensure that any fear is minimized, and your performance maximized.

As with everything, practice makes perfect – your memory will not improve unless you work at it. Shopping lists may serve as a reminder when you get to the supermarket, but you must remember to take the list along in the first place! The memory tips outlined in this section will become second nature if you make a little time to tackle them properly. You will then be able to trust your memory as much as it deserves. People often say, rightly, that the brain is far more intricate than any computer, so, unless you use and service it regularly, you can never get the most from it.

See For Yourself

Assuming that you have remembered what you have just read, your memory should already be able to put into practice some of what it has learned. Tackling the tests below will show you how straightforward the memory techniques outlined above really are, while giving you an opportunity to devise simple methods of your own. The omission of a scoring system here is deliberate – you have already established how effective your basic memory skills are. This is only the start of a promising future for your memory. Soon, your improved performance will say it all.

Spot the Difference

Try tackling this game of spot the difference. First cover up the picture below right. Your task is to study the picture top right for no more than 1 minute, trying to absorb every detail. Now cover the one at the top and look at the slightly different version at the bottom. What are the differences? There is no time limit, but your short-term memory deteriorates with time so the differences are unlikely to seem so obvious after a minute or two.

Memorizing a List – Against the Clock

Now imagine that you've discovered an antique trunk full of all kinds of objects, in the depths of a wild forest. It has obviously been hidden there, undiscovered, for decades. You suddenly notice that, in your excitement, you have lagged far behind your companions, and desperately try to memorize the collection so that you can relate what you saw when you finally catch up. You know that you only have a couple of minutes to spare, or you will lose your friends completely, so concentrate, and see what you can remember after the five minutes that it will take you to rejoin your crowd.

Number-crunching

Spend two minutes studying the table of numbers below before covering it up and trying to reproduce it yourself. Remember that simple repetition techniques may not be sufficient to help you.

2	6	6	1
3	4	2	6
6	3	6	0
4	2	1	8

Self-assessment quiz

Your score:

20-33 Your memory seems to be letting you down, and could well benefit from some of the advice offered later on. For example, try using written reminders as a back-up aid. Perhaps it is actually your lifestyle that is to blame. Your life may be so hectic that you are simply placing too much strain on your poor old memory.

34-47 You appear to have a fairly reliable memory, with the occasional lapse from time to time. Learning a few useful techniques will help to heighten your memory skills further, especially when it comes to remembering things with greater accuracy.
48-60 Congratulations – your memory is in pretty good shape. You seldom forget things, perhaps largely as a result of a well-organized lifestyle. Read on to identify any more specific deficiencies, and to find out how you can improve your memory power even further.

Number Memory

Your score (for the longer number lines)

1-4 Poor. Although you are below average now, however, there is plenty you can do to raise your scores.

5-7 Average. Your number memory is very much like most people's – which means that there's room for a little improvement.

8-10 Outstanding. Your short-term numerical memory serves you very well. Perhaps it's time to look at other areas of your memory skills, such as your visual memory.

Visual Memory

Objects connected with the head and face

Your score:

1-7 Poor. The memory aids detailed later on will point you in the right direction.

8-10 Average. Your visual memory is pretty efficient, but you can still benefit from further practice.

11-12 Outstanding. Your visual memory is a major asset.

Playing the System

It is unlikely that you met with much success. But careful study reveals that the words "dainty elephants" are trapped in the triangle as you read right to left, starting from the bottom right. Reproducing the letter triangle now is no problem.

Memorizing a list – against the clock

Possible memorizing methods include the mnemonic system of moving through a scene; use of rhyme, although time is limited; and attaching words or images to the items.

Number Crunching

Suggested memorizing method: the diagonals read 2, 4, 6, 8 and 1, 2, 3, 4; there is a double 6 in the top row and a 6 on either side. Now just fill in the gaps so that each column adds up to 15.

Putting Names to Faces

Your score

0-13 Poor. You need to work through a few memory tips and techniques in order to exploit your potential.

14-20 Good. Keep working on your memory skills to improve even further.

21-24 Excellent. Your memory seems to cope pretty well with the tricky combination of word lists and visual images.

Spot the Difference

1 Swimming costume on child was striped in left picture, but spotty right
2 Bucket is missing
3 Mum's sunglasses have been removed
4 One less boat is visible on the water
5 The windsurfer has no board
6 Part of the sandcastle is missing
7 The prominent cloud on the left is a different shape
8 The pattern on the beach-towel has changed
9 The fair-haired child now has dark hair
10 Dad was sitting on deckchair; he is now sitting on a sun-lounger
11 The waves are now capped with white foam
12 The vehicle pulled up at the back of the beach is different on right

You may not find it useful to apply any particular method here – instead, try focusing your attention by describing the images out loud or connecting individual features with past experience or even certain words. Hopefully, you will feel that your visual memory has a new heightened awareness.

ASSESS YOURSELF

Reading Skills

Without basic literacy, everyday life can turn into a series of insurmountable hurdles. Having a strong command of language and reading skills unlocks the gate to a much more stimulating and rewarding world. Read on to see how you fare.

Test Your Wordpower

Find the definitions that most closely correspond to the following words.

polemic

a. having electric charges
b. extreme cold
c. controversial
d. at a height

fardel

a. agricultural tool
b. burden
c. remote place
d. obese

3 objurgate

a. reprimand

b. cancel

c. replace

d. urge

4 extemporaneous

a. done without preparation

b. at the same time as

c. temporary

d. done in advance

5 pilose

a. criminal activity

b. drug addiction

c. covered with hair

d. cheerful

6 juvenescence

a. period of study

b. composition

c. state of complete elation

d. immaturity

ASSESS YOURSELF

7 voluble

a. talkative

b. gullible

c. generous

d. overflowing

8 julep

a. member of the mint family

b. type of drink

c. encouragement

d. children's game

9 anneal

a. heat metal or glass to toughen it

b. treat wound

c. apply protective covering

d. make member of a royal order

10 oleaginous

a. prehistoric

b. shiny

c. deceitful

d. oily or greasy

11 lustrate

a. add extra diagrams

b. perform ritual purification

c. robust fitness

d. enthuse

12 unguent

a. stilted and hesitant

b. ointment

c. African hunter

d. strong adhesive

13 brio

a. rivalry

b. the "spirit of the age"

c. verve and vivacity

d. arrogance

14 cabochon

a. rank in the French army

b. type of wheel common in ceremonial carriages

c. polished gem without facets

d. clever trick

15 **cicerone**

a. person lacking courage

b. conductor of sightseers

c. heat-loving insect

d. ancient temple

16 **rondo**

a. piece of music

b. Italian pasta dish

c. lively dance

d. poem of 10 or 13 lines

17 **tamarin**

a. evergreen tree

b. musical instrument

c. tropical fruit

d. South American monkey

18 **mettle**

a. conductor of heat

b. courage

c. interfere

d. weld together

19 **sibilant**

a. with a hissing sound

b. close family relation

c. family reunion

d. ecstasy

20 **eclogue**

a. environmental study

b. short poem

c. position of the moon

d. general discussion

Playing the Detective

Your task here is to find the intruder among the following groups of words.

1

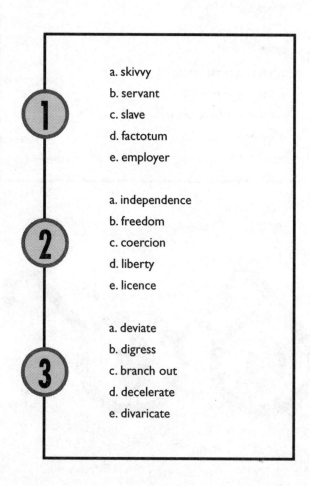

a. skivvy
b. servant
c. slave
d. factotum
e. employer

2

a. independence
b. freedom
c. coercion
d. liberty
e. licence

3

a. deviate
b. digress
c. branch out
d. decelerate
e. divaricate

4

a. initiate

b. procrastinate

c. delay

d. put off

e. postpone

5

a. vigilance

b. observation

c. watchfulness

d. inertia

e. invigilation

6

a. curiosity

b. zeal

c. nonchalance

d. officiousness

e. interest

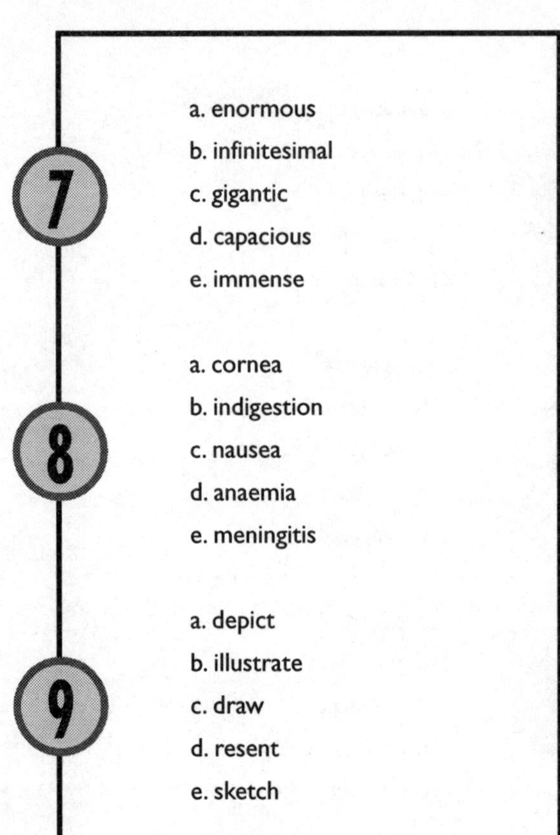

7

a. enormous
b. infinitesimal
c. gigantic
d. capacious
e. immense

8

a. cornea
b. indigestion
c. nausea
d. anaemia
e. meningitis

9

a. depict
b. illustrate
c. draw
d. resent
e. sketch

10

a. lingo
b. dialect
c. idiom
d. parlance
e. auditory

11

a. versatility
b. ambidextrousness
c. flexibility
d. adaptability
e. conductibility

12

a. insatiable
b. gluttonous
c. vivacious
d. devouring
e. voracious

Speed Reading

Studies have shown that faster reading enhances learning and memory skills, as well as having the obvious benefit of saving time. Use the following passage to test your reading skills. All you need are a watch with a second hand to time yourself and a pen to record your starting and finishing times. Take care to read as you would normally – the aim here is to test your current ability, enabling you to determine how far you need to improve.

After timing your reading of the passage, tackle the multiple-choice comprehension test. Do this without referring to the passage at all, selecting the statement that most closely corresponds to the text.

The Text

Eugène Boudin (1824-1898) is renowned for the many beach scenes he painted at Trouville, on the coast of Normandy in France. Coastal themes dominated his prolific output, which included almost 4,000 oil paintings. Having had a childhood strongly influenced by the sea, this lifelong artistic interest comes as little surprise.

He was born at Honfleur, a seaside town where Eugène's father Leonard had followed the tradition of countless Honfleur men before him by becoming a sailor. Leonard Boudin began his apprenticeship for the navy at the tender age of 11, later acting as a gunner in battles on the high seas against the English. He then swapped his bullets for a fishing rod, and began to earn a living fishing for cod. After eight years of marriage, Louis-Eugène was born on the 12th of July, 1824.

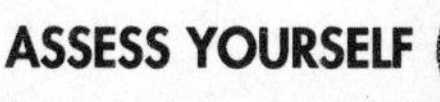

Early Promise

Leonard Boudin's many years at sea enabled him to take charge of a small vessel trading between Rouen and Honfleur. His talented son was soon on board working as a cabin boy, and passed the time during breaks from his tasks by sketching. Even from a young age, Eugène Boudin was uplifted and inspired by life on the water.

Following a move to Le Havre in 1835, where his father took up a new shipping job, Eugène began to attend a school run by priests. Here, his artistic talents flourished. At the age of 12, however, this came to an abrupt end when Leonard decided to curtail his son's education and the boy began work as a printer's clerk in Le Havre. He then moved on to a job in a stationer's, where he worked his way up and became the owner's secretary. Despite offering little prospect of further promotion, Eugène received a gift from the owner of this stationer's that would have a vital influence on him: his first paintbox.

A New Era Dawns

In 1838, the development of steamship traffic at this time enabled Leonard to find work on a steamer called *Le Français*, which frequented Honfleur and Le Havre. Eugène's mother also took to the seas, working as a stewardess on steamships in the area. Yet neither his parents' occupations, nor his early experience on the ocean, stimulated any desire in Eugène to follow a similar path. Instead, he formed a partnership with a foreman who had also worked for Lemasle, the stationers at which Eugène had previously been employed. This partnership gave birth to a new stationer's shop, and allowed Eugène to enjoy the work of visiting artists whose pictures they framed and displayed.

The personal contact that Boudin maintained with these artists and their work made him determined to become a painter himself. Despite words of warning offered by the artist Jean-François Millet about the precariousness of such a profession, Boudin carried on regardless. After arguing with his partner Jean Archer, in 1846, Boudin left their shop to embark on a life devoted to the art he loved. It was this powerful devotion alone that would keep him going through the difficult years that lay ahead.

The Lure of the Sea

The hypnotic magic of the open water came to rule Boudin's otherwise miserable struggle to survive, and he often worked in the open air, overlooking the sea. Extremely modest sales of his work were enough to fuel his passion for painting, and his passion to learn more about the great masters.

Le Havre's offerings were limited – what Boudin needed to quench his thirst for knowledge was Paris, with its museums and stimulating artistic life. A year after ending his partnership, Boudin's scrimping and saving paid off and he arrived in Paris. What awaited him was not the land of his dreams – survival in the city was, in many ways, more of a struggle than the provincial life that he was accustomed to. Boudin did, however, spend endless hours studying the paintings he so revered, which taught him a great deal but also filled him with despair at what he saw as his own inadequacy. This despondency would remain with him throughout his artistic life.

Any travel was a large undertaking for a man so attached to his native land. Boudin's trip around Belgium and northern France was purely the result of a certain Baron Taylor, whose interest in art led him to run several societies that helped aspiring artists who needed financial support. This support helped all of the parties concerned: while Boudin toured around displaying his work, he sold lottery tickets in aid of artists in a similar situation to himself.

Recognition at Last

Boudin continued to paint – seascapes, still lifes and copies of works by the great masters. His copies proved to be particularly profitable, largely due to commissions from Baron Taylor. His efforts were finally put on show properly for the first time in 1850, after his return to Le Havre. The exhibition enabled him to sell two of his paintings, bought by the purchasing committee of the art-loving society responsible for organizing the exhibition in the first place. It was from this society that Boudin received a grant of 3,600 francs, over three years. After remaining in Paris up to 1854, he was finally able to leave the confines of the capital to return to the pleasures of Le Havre, free to embark on his future career.

ASSESS YOURSELF

Comprehension

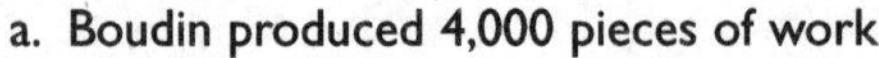

1

a. Boudin produced 4,000 pieces of work.
b. Boudin created just under 4,000 paintings on a coastal theme.
c. His total output included almost 4,000 oil paintings.

2

a. Before departing for Paris, Boudin enjoyed an extravagant lifestyle.
b. Boudin saved for a considerable time before leaving for Paris.
c. A grant funded Boudin's first trip to Paris.

3

a. Eugène Boudin's first job was at sea.
b. Eugène Boudin trained as a gunner.
c. Eugène Boudin started work when he was 12 years old.

4

a. Lemasle provided Eugène with his first set of paints.
b. Eugène's father was responsible for his first encounter with the world of painting.
c. Eugène was given his first box of paints while at a school run by priests.

5

a. Boudin's first exhibition took place in Paris.
b. The first significant exhibition of Boudin's paintings was in Le Havre.
c. Boudin never had a proper display of his work.

6

a. Leonard Boudin worked on the first steamship.
b. Leonard Boudin found work during the rise in the use of steamships.
c. Leonard Boudin helped develop the use of steamships.

7

a. Eugène was always confident about his work.
b. Eugène continually criticized his own work.
c. Eugène became known as an art critic.

8

a. Much of Eugène's work stemmed from his study of the sea.
b. As a young man, Eugène dreamed of a career on the waves.
c. Eugène preferred to work indoors.

9

a. Baron Taylor purchased Eugène's early still lifes.
b. Eugène's three-year stay in Paris was financed by Baron Taylor.
c. Eugène was commissioned by the Baron to make copies of works by the great masters.

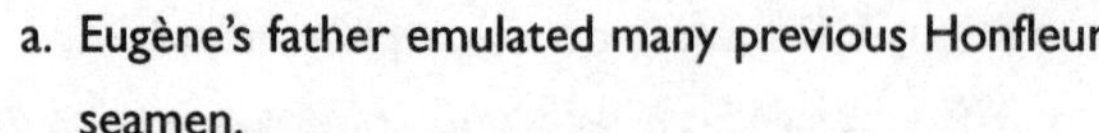

a. Eugène's father emulated many previous Honfleur seamen.

b. Eugène was born in Le Havre.

c. Eugène was born in Trouville.

An estimated 40% of adults across the world are said to be unable to read. Reading is not just a question of making a concentrated effort to recognize a series of visual symbols. It also becomes an integral part of the way we process information, enabling us to read words quicker than we could say them – we've all had the experience of the eyes being swifter than the tongue.

In Control

In general terms, the processing of language is controlled by the left half of the brain. Within this half, specific regions are responsible for different types of language manipulation. Being able to write, and the ability to control your voice, stems from processes that take place in the frontal lobe. Damage to the parietal lobe, toward the back of the brain, can result in alexia, a condition where it becomes difficult to read words without confusing the letters. The temporal lobe, located by the ear, and the outer layer of the parietal lobe, control the capacity to understand what it being said to us. Harming these areas can result in deafness – if this happens to a child, learning to read can be an upward struggle.

The Process of Reading

We all appreciate that efficient reading skills can extend our understanding and vocabulary, while a poor reading technique and selection of reading matter can substantially hinder our progress. Focusing exclusively on reading as rapidly as possible often results in a failure to grasp the meaning of the material, and the reader may need to begin all over again. The ideal reading technique involves the use of careful, considered skimming strategies. For example, an initial scan of a piece of text gives the reader a broad overview, enabling the brain to focus properly on the general subject matter. Just as the body needs warming up before vigorous exercise, so too does the mind.

The Eyes Have It

Different reading techniques are often linked to eye movement. Studies have shown how reading requires a continual, rapid cycle of stops and starts, the eyes focusing suddenly on a batch of letters before swooping on to the next batch. Due to the brain's preference for chunks of information, as opposed to single bits, the more words that can be absorbed at a glance, the easier and quicker it is to learn.

The overview obtained by effective skimming can make a huge difference to your powers of comprehension and recall. There is no specific scanning method – the eyes may wander vertically, horizontally and diagonally across the page, focusing on individual key words, phrases and titles. A page may be scanned in anything from 2 to 20 seconds. The speed and technique is unique to each individual, as are the resulting benefits.

Perhaps most importantly, skimming can lessen the fear that many people feel when reading something new. Escaping the feeling that you must concentrate equally on every word helps to set the mind at ease. The more relaxed reading that will follow on from this makes the entire process altogether more rewarding.

Flexibility is the Key

Whatever your reading speed, a good reader needs to maintain a flexible approach. Obviously, a complicated passage requires greater study, with slower reading and less text skimmed or skipped. It has been shown that fast readers may study at a pace similar to slower workers in such sections, but more efficient reading and scanning of less important passages enables their overall speed to be maintained.

The major key to efficient retention and recall of written information is understanding, not merely being able to repeat something "parrot-fashion." If you have a high level of

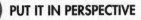

understanding, the brain stays sharply focused on the subject matter and you will find it far easier to read quickly. The foundation stones of effective understanding and efficient reading technique are:

- The ability to relate individual words and sentences to the context as a whole
- Maintaining and focusing your interest by taking breaks, making notes, perhaps referring to other texts, making more heavy-going material accessible by linking it with other subjects that you enjoy more
- Keeping fresh by pausing every so often

Reading can provide us with a whole world of fascinating education and enjoyment – but only if you learn to read actively, with a questioning mind, using it as a springboard for finding out even more.

There are all kinds of easy ways in which you can improve your reading skills.

Making the Most of Your Daily Read

Newspapers provide an invaluable source of reading material, often helping us to improve both our vocabulary range and our speed reading skills. Delving into a range of different newspapers can make us more aware of the different styles of language that are effective in different situations, as well as providing interest and variety. Scanning through a paper helps you to locate articles of immediate interest, improving your ability to focus on what is strictly relevant, and discarding what isn't.

Increasing Your Speeds

Now that you have a general notion of your reading speed, you can formulate a plan of self-improvement. For example, try selecting an article of approximately 1,000 words. Time how long it takes you to read this, and then write a brief summary of the piece to test your overall comprehension. Try to assess yourself as honestly as possible, or you will gain little from the exercise. Find your reading speed per minute by following the process explained on page 43: count the number of words in the article, multiply it by 60, and divide this by your time in seconds. A reasonable amount of practice should result in an increased speed of around 100.

Test Your Scanning Abilities

The exercise overleaf is designed to test your ability to scan a page for the most important information, giving you greater understanding and improved reading efficiency. Your task is to work through each line, glancing at the first group of letters, then marking the position of its twin, positioned somewhere else in each line. As you work through, the letter groups get larger. A metronome may help you to maintain speed – set the pace to correspond with the time it takes you to get through one of the first lines. Trying to stick to this rhythm as you progress will help you to broaden the range of characters your eyes can take in within a given time.

BA	GU	B C	ST	IN	LK	BA	AA
OJ	LP	TG	BC	SE	OJ	QJ	BR
CT	IP	CT	EY	KB	FG	TH	NO
LF	YU	BU	LF	UB	DY	IH	BK
VT	VT	KI	CT	IU	PV	EJ	OG
UI	HD	TB	LK	OG	CR	UM	UI
DE	YU	JU	KI	DE	SG	KU	OL
MO	DT	MO	RT	UH	MV	DE	YG
CX	TE	JH	JI	CX	KT	CT	EC
OT	GY	UI	BF	TD	OT	NU	OP
CV	GT	CV	JY	IJ	OM	LP	DW
KP	HU	TE	PK	KP	RT	VD	IN
CT	ES	WI	UN	HO	PL	BC	CT
BY	UI	JN	BY	ER	OJ	LN	CT
VY	IO	FT	PO	JH	CT	WS	VY
UO	TF	ER	VT	DY	UO	KH	DT
PO	PN	UT	FY	IN	PO	HY	ER
NU	TY	MI	OP	MV	FT	ED	NU
BU	TI	OP	MI	YU	BU	DT	BY
VY	ER	VY	UO	JO	PL	MU	YU

TEST IT OUT

BYT	CRU	OPK	BNT	UIO	TYD	BYT	UIM
VHI	FTY	VSR	EDI	KOM	VHI	DTW	QAU
MOL	BYR	MOL	PHI	TBD	YUI	NOF	GHI
WXT	GUE	WAI	HUB	WXT	UBI	MOP	HIM
EUT	IUY	EUT	GON	BIE	EUF	YBI	UIO
BJD	YRU	DFG	IOU	NUI	VHT	DRT	BJD
LPB	UTD	CTS	HIM	LPB	CTE	UGM	NIT
NIB	HUI	DTE	CUG	NIB	PKT	DEA	JIB
YTE	MIT	UI	HFR	YTE	CFT	LOP	YUI
VTY	UIO	VTY	RSE	YTU	HJI	NPO	MIG
CTY	UIO	JNR	ERT	VJU	CSE	RTF	CTY
IOH	CTE	UIV	SJW	TFA	IOH	OPB	CRA
GYM	KOI	VZE	GYM	VUS	WQA	VRI	OPL
NID	RYG	NIA	WQE	RCG	IOM	NID	PLF
VUE	KOP	LFE	ZPO	VUE	ASU	REL	BUI
NZE	RTY	IGS	BOP	LMV	STQ	UOI	NZE
QRT	UYF	BHU	PAS	LGR	WQD	QRT	UIV
BDT	GUA	BDT	OPG	UTW	DFC	BZH	JUO
CAR	CAR	TYU	CGQ	IGS	PLN	ETU	CAT
MKE	UTV	HSM	MKI	VHA	TEC	MKE	IUB

MAOW VYSE YYJV MAOW UYRV MOPD GTEH NIPL
BIDT FTEY NUIO MODE UYIB BIDT YUIN MPLY
SDWR YUIO JCEN NJOM NSTR KOPB MODT SDWR
MPLD UITB XDRW YUIB MKOR YUIJ MPLD REWY
CSTW ITHB VGIR CSTW HJIM MPLH UIOD ETUB
NUOM JHGD RYUV NUIE NUOM KPLG TYIC EYYC
BUET HUIP BUET DEAU IJFO MIFT ECSU INFT
MPLG YRWE BHIP MOPD RTUO MPLG YUID RTUV
BUTE IOHN TETY BUTE TYIF JKKR RTUV NOIY
VDTE TYUB NIOF TYIU NOPF VDTE TYIB MIOO
NDAN RTIJ BHIL PFTW RUVJ NDAN KOPL NCTT
OPLM TPKG AHUI OPLM VTSR TYUO MOJU FTUO
BHDQ YIIB GIUM VYUO BUSE YUON BHDQ OKMG
PCZE TUOB CJOR OMVB TDEY PCZE IONF WRUJ
FALK IOGD GTAF UFAK LUIU FALK OPHC EOHF
VHIF GYTI BHRE OIHF JTEF LKUH VHIF IOKH
HDEI OPKV DSHE TUIB HDEI OPLM VSIH KYVL
UPAI UPAI MKOF EROB CTSR YIOJ BAGU OMAK
LJST YIHB LJST HUOO NCTW TYIB MKSY OPNC
BAJI YUOK BGST UPKN BAJI PLBD TUOB GHAJ

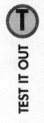

TEST IT OUT

CEWIQ	OPKLC	CEWIQ	LNVK	STUMD	VUSWD	TRUGF	BIDMF
MSIFO	VGJOD	JBHUS	TYUKH	GHHTR	MSIFO	FGHJT	DRFUI
AVGHJ	TINBM	FTUUY	GHUIO	AVGHJ	OPOLM	GYUIU	VTYEJ
BUDTE	BHILJ	VBHYR	HIUJN	KLIPO	VHGUR	HJIOM	BUDTE
VHUIO	KOOPJ	DFTTR	NKOLK	VHUIO	PLVGY	RTJIO	CGHJK
ADFTT	UOIJK	MLKOI	ADFTT	UOINV	GYIOK	BHJTR	IOONF
KGUYR	HGUIM	GHJUY	TYTFJ	IOIHH	RTUYB	KGUYR	BVHUT
FAJDE	TYIKM	VHJKM	RTIOC	FAJDE	YIUON	FKJYM	FHTHM
LVGSD	YUIHV	KIOUI	FTIUB	LPFES	LVGSD	YIOKG	RTIJF
AMOPH	GHUII	NJAIU	YUIOK	AMOPH	DRQWT	PIREV	NJIUT
SGUAI	YGERI	OPJHF	SGUAI	PLMGR	UIOMF	BTGYO	BHTJM
NAGSH	KOLIU	HJSKA	HJIUY	IOIMN	NAGSH	UOJMN	GHJAY
LSNXH	YUIOS	BNJSY	KYIAO	BHJSU	LSNXH	UIAOM	SGETQ
ANSHR	TYAIO	NBSFT	TAIJN	ANSHR	UIOSK	BBBSG	JAJYS
OITFS	HTYEW	RYUOA	OGABS	HSYRS	OITFS	NHGSK	OPPAN
ERLAE	HSOAM	HGSYK	ERLAE	JOPMF	PAFST	YUIOS	BAHJO
SJDHF	SJDHF	UIOPK	SKYRE	JIOMG	FAVHJ	KLPOO	BFSTY
LANSH	JIOIT	GTYJN	KOOGR	LANSH	UIOPK	BFRTY	NGHOK
IWTQY	MAHST	JHQHG	IWTQY	IOISH	NMAJS	NNSJS	USIOA
JSHWW	JSHWW	YYIOP	JLFSW	QDTUO	NFSTT	YUIOK	GSFSK

You can devise similar tests yourself, using letters, numbers or other symbols. Alternatively, try skimming text for a particular (common) word. A conscious effort to read faster and skim better will inevitably improve your skills without a huge amount of effort.

Stretch Your Wordpower

To extend your vocabulary, you will find numerous written tests similar to those in the self-assessment section in other books of this nature. However, the general context of the word is often missing in such tests. Wider reading of a challenging nature, exploiting the full range of books, magazines and newspapers, will help you to develop a more accurate and varied vocabulary.

When writing, having a thesaurus and dictionary to hand provides instant access to a language goldmine. Spelling difficulties can be lessened by examining the word visually – letting your mind absorb the shape, size and quantity of letters. Play around with the word mentally, creating its own identity in your mind. Stimulating the mind in these ways will also help to unlock all kinds of words that you had forgotten you even knew!

Knowledge of some common Latin, Greek and English prefixes and suffixes is always helpful when you don't have a dictionary to hand, because it allows you to make informed guesses about word meanings. A brief list follows.

TEST IT OUT

PREFIX STEM AND EXAMPLE	DEFINITION OF PREFIX	SUFFIX STEM AND EXAMPLE	DEFINITION OF SUFFIX
ab-stract	away from	enjoy-able	capable of
ad-jacent	next to/towards	cardi-ac	pertaining to
an-aphrodisiac	not/without	advant-age	action/locality
ante-date	before	annu-al	pertaining to
anti-freeze	opposing/against	abund-ance	state/action
arch-angel	principal	pleas-ant	causing/performing action
auto-biography	self	secret-ary	dealing with/
bene-volent	well		place for
bi-focal	twice	anim-ate	cause to be
bio-logy	life	arti-cle	indicating smallness
cent-enary	one hundred	wis-dom	power/condition
centi-grade	one hundreth	wax-en	made of
circum-ference	around	kitt-en	small
com-pose	together/with	acqu-eous	pertaining to
con-tain	together/with	sing-er	belonging to
contra-vene	against	conval-escent	steadily becoming
de-compose	reversal	coni-ferous	bearing
demi-god	half	fanci-ful	full of
dia-meter	through/during	beauti-fy	to make
dis-like	reversal	widow-hood	state/condition
ex-hale	out of	rept-ile	capable of being
extra-sensory	outside/beyond	redd-ish	relationship/similarity
fore-see	before		

Prefix stem and example	Definition of prefix	Suffix stem and example	Definition of suffix
hemi-sphere	half	scept-ism	state/system
homo-logous	same	pharmac-ist	one who does
inter-act	between	hepat-itis	medical: inflammation
intro-spection	inside/into	capabil-ity	state/quality
mal-evolent	bad	civil-ize	to make/act
mega-lopolis	great	gut-less	free from/lacking
micro-dot	small	socio-logy	doctrine/knowledge
mis-fit	wrongly	amuse-ment	state/act of
mono-logue	single/one	thermo-meter	measure of
non-sense	not	matri-mony	condition
ob-struct	in the way	vigil-ance	state/condition
para-graph	beside/near	vigil-ancy	state/quality
per-forate	through	cub-oid	resembling
peri-meter	around/about	conduct-or	one who/thing which
poly-gon	many/much		
post-orbital	after	verb-ose	full of
pre-eminant	before	garrul-ous	full of
pro-vide	before/in front	tele-scope	aid to sight
pseudo-nym	false	censor-ship	state/office of
retro-active	back/backwards	trouble-some	full of/like
semi-breve	half	young-ster	one who/association
sub-editor	under/beneath		
super-sonic	above/over	fanta-sy	state
syn-thesis	with/together	percep-tion	abtract state
tele-cast	distant/far	apti-tude	state/degree of
trans-atlantic	across/beyond	glob-ule	small
ultra-marine	beyond	back-ward	direction
uni-lateral	one	clock-wise	direction/manner
vice-president	in place of	murk-y	condition

Setting attainable goals over a regular course of reading should encourage you to practice and lead to great improvement. Challenge your mind constantly – it needs to be well-nourished, and not simply fed on junk food.

Test Your Wordpower

Answers

1.c 2.b 3.a 4.a 5.c 6.d 7.a 8.b 9.a 10.d

11.b 12.b 13.c 14.c 15.b 16.a 17.d 18.b 19.a 20.b

Your Score

0-5: Poor. You've probably just got a little lazy over the years – make improving your vocabulary a priority now and you'll soon see what a difference it can make.

6-10: Average. You, too, will benefit from broader knowledge.

11-15: Very good. But keep trying even harder.

16-20: Excellent.

Playing the Detective

Answers

1.e 2.c 3.d 4.a 5.d 6.c

7.b 8.a 9.d 10.e 11.e 12.c

Your Score

Below 6	Poor. But that just means plenty of room for improvement.
7 or 8	Average. Quite acceptable range – keep working on it.
9 or 10	Pretty good. You have a wide vocabulary at your disposal.
11 or 12	Excellent. Although you can never know enough where words are concerned.

Speed Reading

Comprehension:

Answers

1.c 2.b 3.a 4.a 5.b

6.b 7.b 8.a 9.c 10.a

Your Score

Under 7 statements correct: You are perhaps not concentrating as well as you could, or are simply reading too quickly.

7 or more correct: You have a fairly satisfactory level of comprehension – but it could always be better!

To calculate your reading speed:

1. Multiply the number of words in the passage by the number of seconds in an hour, which in this case would be 50,400 (840 x 60).

2. Divide 50,400 by the total number of seconds it took you to read the passage.

So, with a total reading time of 206 seconds, your reading speed would be 245 words per minute.

Your Score

245 words per minute is a fairly average score. A score of around 200 could certainly do with a bit of work, while one of 600 is pretty exceptional.

Understanding Numbers

The following tests give you the opportunity to assess your numerical skills using the four basic mathematical operations – addition, subtraction, multiplication and division. You have up to 90 minutes to work through the questions. After assessing your skills, read on to discover how to make the numbers in your life work for you.

1. Replace the question marks to make the string of calculations complete.

		27	+	?	=	71
						×
84	-	?	=	55		3
=				+		=
?		124	=	?		?
×						-
12	=	?	÷	?	=	69

2. During a day out shopping for a forthcoming business trip, Sandra bought 12 boxes of Belgian chocolates, priced at $7 each, for which she handed over a money order already made out for $100. She then added the change to the sum of 7 $50 bills and 7 loose dollar bills she had in her wallet. After buying 4 tickets to a show, costing $33 each, how much money did Sandra have left over?

3. Study the triangles to find the recurring pattern that will enable you to replace the letters with the correct figures.

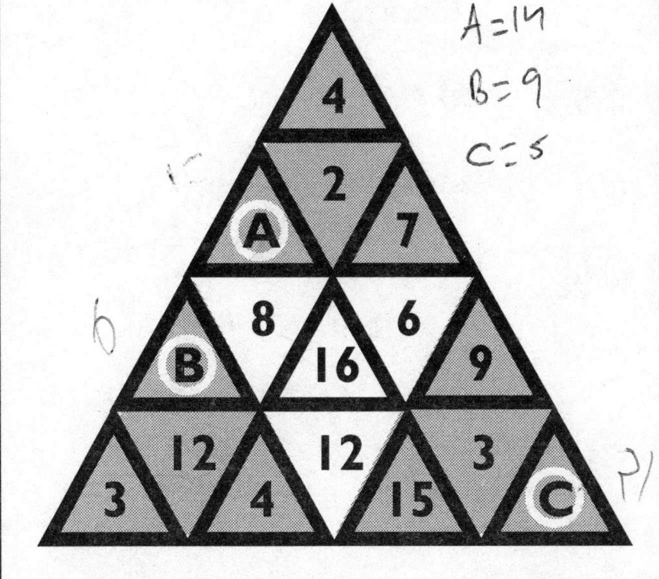

ASSESS YOURSELF

ASSESS YOURSELF

4. If:

A is a third of B

A = 3C – 4

B = 8 + 5C

then what value does C have?

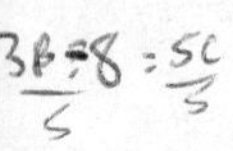

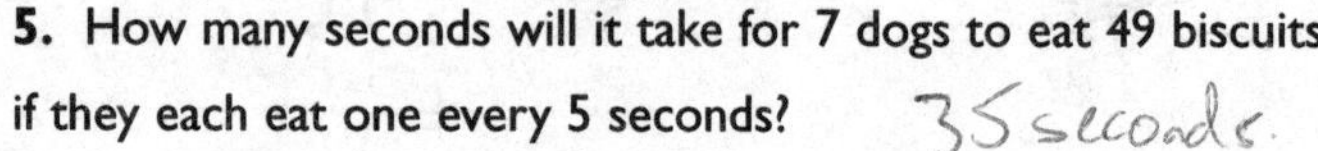

5. How many seconds will it take for 7 dogs to eat 49 biscuits if they each eat one every 5 seconds?

6. What number comes next in each of the sequences below?

a) 160, 40, 10, ?

b) 7, 22, 67, ?

c) 68, 36, 20, 12, ?

d) 145, 134, 122, 109, ?

e) 33, 24, 34, 23, ?

7. What number replaces the question mark below the grid?

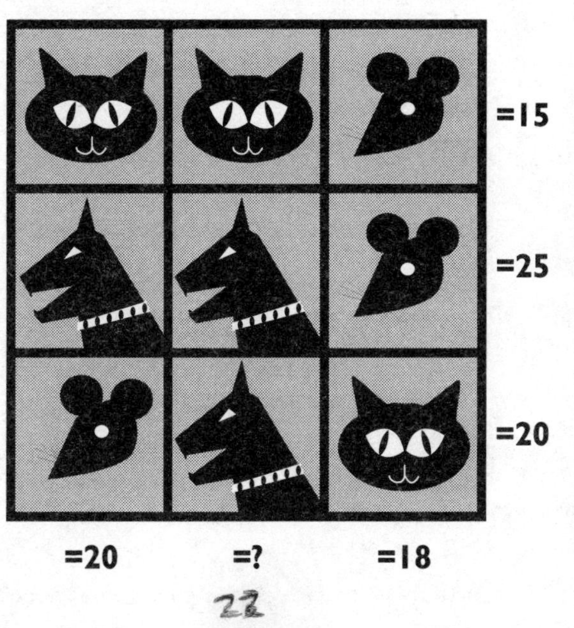

8. How far does the Adams family have to travel to visit their relations if they drive at 60 mph for 20 minutes, spend 3½ hours at a constant 75 mph, and drive for the last 25 minutes at a speed of 40 mph, during which time they stop for 2 minutes to seek directions?

9. Break up each of the following series of numbers, using 2 or 3 of the basic mathematical operations.

a) 2 2 2 2 2 = 66

b) 4 4 4 4 4 = 55

c) 7 7 7 7 7 = 22

d) 6 6 6 6 6 = 11

e) 3 3 3 3 3 = 66

10. If P is half of Q when Q equals the square root of 3 dozen, then what is the numerical value of P?

11. At a birthday party, each child is given some chocolates. There are 6 five-year-olds, 6 six-year-olds and 6 seven-year-olds present. If each child receives 3 times as many chocolates as their age in years, how many chocolates are handed out altogether?

12. Which symbol would balance the third scale?

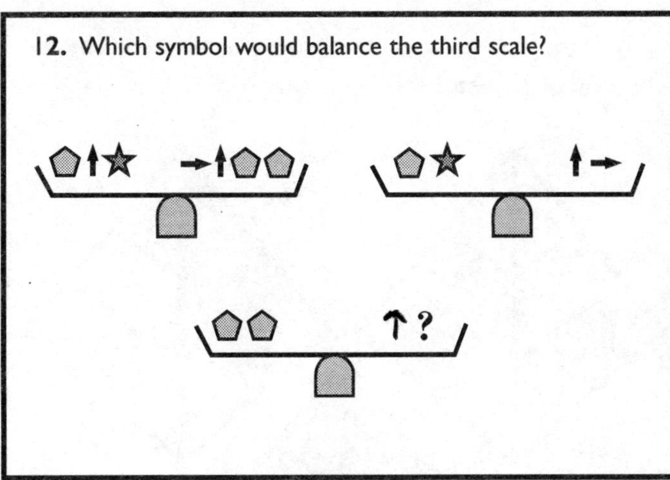

13. If Z is the square of 8, what is X if X is 3 times the value of Y, which is a quarter of Z?

14. On average, 5% of pupils at a particular school are absent each day. With 3 classes of 24, 4 classes of 27 and 5 classes of 32, how many children are expected to attend each day?

15. A clock correctly reads 9:30 on one particular Saturday morning, but then starts to run too fast, gaining 4 minutes each hour. What is the actual time when the clock displays 5 p.m.?

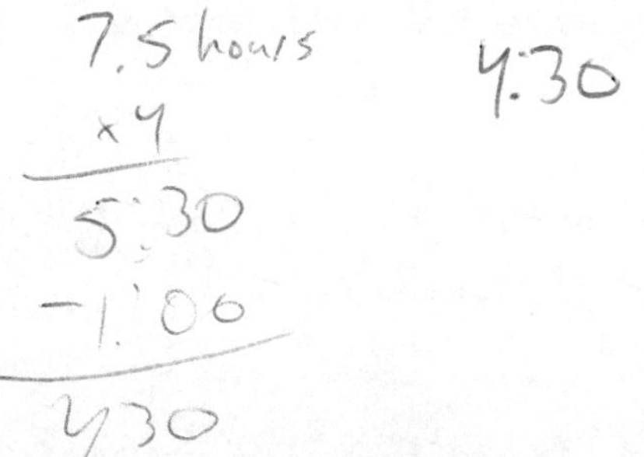

16. Study the 3 pyramids to discover the correct numerical value of each question mark.

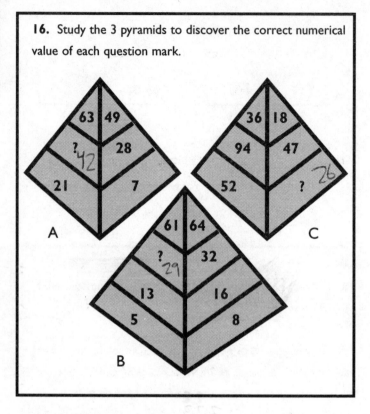

A: 63, 49, ?, 28, 21, 7

B: 61, 64, ?, 32, 13, 16, 5, 8

C: 36, 18, 94, 47, 52, ?

17. Janine invests \$200 on January 1st each year in a savings account for her granddaughter. Annual interest of 10% is earned on all the money, payable on December 31st. How much money is in the account on January 2nd in the third year of the account?

18. How much is M worth if 8M – 3N = 29 and 5N – 13 = 32?

19. A desk-making workshop is held one weekend, and various teams from the north and south of the area are taking part. Glue is needed to make these desks. If 60% of the 15 northern teams and 55% of the 20 southern teams managed to obtain it, how many teams are left without glue?

20. According to the other 2 pictures, how many birds do the 3 clouds lack?

21. What do S and T equal if 4R = 6S = 8T and 7R = 42?

22. A cube-shaped swimming pool is drained to change the water. The water had a depth of exactly 5 feet. How long will it take to empty the pool if the water level decreases by 3 inches every 4 minutes?

> **Multiplication is vexation,**
> **Division is as bad;**
> **The rule of three doth puzzle me, And practice drives me mad.**
>
> **(Anon.)**

If the prospect of confronting a page crammed with figures makes you shudder, you are not alone. Numbers can fill the most literate and educated of people with fear, but you will soon discover that most of these fears are groundless.

After working through the self-assessment section, you may already have realized that most of the tests are much simpler than they first appeared. Consider the shopping problem. Delete all the extraneous text and you are left with a few basic figures from which a simple series of calculations lead you to the answer.

PUT IT IN PERSPECTIVE

The most important things to remember when dealing with numbers are:

- Don't panic

- Keep things simple

Whether attempting problems like the ones included here, or sifting through mounds of paperwork to work out your disposable income, keep the data as simple and well organized as possible.

Building Barriers

We are bombarded with numbers in one form or another from a very young age. As children, we can easily work out that one of the 6 parts of a certain game is missing or that our pocket money is short by a certain amount. We happily count up to large numbers during a game of hide-and-seek. Yet as soon as numbers are connected with school and work, our previously casual attitude is often transformed.

Once we are criticized for a careless mathematical error, the fear of making further mistakes often causes us to build a complete mental barricade where any numbers are concerned. Such fear inevitably prevents progress, encouraging a loathing for the subject, and a refusal to learn.

The power of your brain cannot be underestimated. You may wonder at the sophistication and speed with which today's computers hurry through complicated calculations, but creating a computer with the abilities of the human mind would be impossible. The size of such a machine would be unmanageable – as would the instruction manual! So have confidence in yourself next time you are faced with pages of calculations. Don't always reach for a calculator – take the opportunity to make your mind work harder, and the practice will soon start to make a difference.

Making Numbers Work for You

Despite the "vexation" that mathematics may provoke, it is actually a simplification of everyday life. Numbers often act as a straightforward code for much more complex ideas, so the notion that you can't tackle them at all would seem to be

completely illogical. How often have you switched on the news to hear a lengthy description of a company's performance that could have been represented far more succinctly by a graph? Of course numbers and statistics can always be manipulated and used to impress – mainly because most people are too afraid of figures to question them. So don't believe another person's calculations as a matter of course – be on your guard!

From building the Great Pyramids to the latest advances in computer technology, mathematics has always played an important part of human life. Each advance has the potential to bring further benefit, so concentrate on making numbers work for you, and don't simply shy away from them.

To do or not to do – that is the question. It is impossible to master any level of mathematics by just reading about it. Being confident with numbers requires practice and experimentation. If the very idea makes you nervous, don't automatically reject it before giving it a go. A little practice can rapidly lead to heartening results. As with any game, you have to learn the rules before you start to play.

The number tips that follow are designed simply as an aid to basic numeracy – it's up to you to decide how far you need to take it.

Multiplication and Division

Does the mere mention of "multiplication tables" bring back some of your least cherished childhood memories, of schooldays filled with endless repetition and tests? If so, don't despair. Multiplication is very useful in everyday life, as you find when you need to work out how much 6 boxes of chocolates at $7 each will cost during a Christmas shopping spree. Chances are, you will tackle the necessary calculations very effectively, because there is no teacher peering over your desk, pressurizing you for an answer; no one ready to laugh at your mistakes. If you take your time, and make a point of working things out in your head, rapid multiplication could soon become second nature.

TEST IT OUT

For simple calculations, a multiplication and division table is provided below for your reference. To multiply two numbers together, go down the column of one until you meet the row of the other to arrive at the answer. So, 6 lots of $7 costs $42. For division, go down the column headed with the smaller number until you find the larger number that is to be divided into. The row number gives the answer. So, if you have 72 inches of timber that you want to divide into 8-inch lengths, working down column 8 until you reach 72 shows that you will have 9 lengths altogether. But if you have 90 inches and still want 8-inch lengths, find the number closest to 90 in column 8 (which is 88) to discover that you can cut 11 complete lengths with 2 inches of timber left over.

	COLUMN													
ROW	**2**	**3**	**4**	**5**	**6**	**7**	**8**	**9**	**10**	**11**	**12**	**13**	**14**	**15**
2	4	6	8	10	12	14	16	18	20	22	24	26	28	30
3	6	9	12	15	18	21	24	27	30	33	36	39	42	45
4	8	12	16	20	24	28	32	36	40	44	48	52	56	60
5	10	15	20	25	30	35	40	45	50	55	60	65	70	75
6	12	18	24	30	36	42	48	54	60	66	72	78	84	90
7	14	21	28	35	42	49	56	63	70	77	84	91	98	105
8	16	24	32	40	48	56	64	72	80	88	96	104	112	120
9	18	27	36	45	54	63	72	81	90	99	108	117	126	135
10	20	30	40	50	60	70	80	90	100	110	120	130	140	150
11	22	33	44	55	66	77	88	99	110	121	132	143	154	165
12	24	36	48	60	72	84	96	108	120	132	144	156	168	180
13	26	39	52	65	78	91	104	117	130	143	156	169	182	195
14	28	42	56	70	84	98	112	126	140	154	168	182	196	210
15	30	45	60	75	90	105	120	135	150	165	180	195	210	225

Sometimes problems can actually be solved more quickly without the use of a table, or even a calculator. This is especially true when dealing with the numbers 5 and 10. For example, if you want to buy 10 notebooks priced at $4.50 each, you will be spending $45:

4.5 x 10 = 45

To multiply a decimal number by 10, all you have to do is move the decimal point one place to the right. If you are working with a whole number, all you have to do is add a nought: 10 boxes each containing 12 pens hold 120 pens in total.

It therefore follows that, to divide by 10, you remove a nought (if there is one) or shift a decimal point one place to the left. Where a whole number such as 45 is concerned, it is sometimes easier to view it as 45.0, so that the position of the decimal point is clear in your mind.

When dealing with the number 5, remind yourself that it is simply half of 10. So, if you are multiplying by 5, add a nought to the relevant number, or shift the decimal point to the right, and then divide by 2. Five of the notebooks priced at $4.50 cost $22.50:

4.5 x 10 = 45

45 ÷ 2 = 22.5

TEST IT OUT

To divide the 120 pens between 5 people is just a case of common sense – doubling 120 and dividing that by 10. Knowing how to multiply a number by 10 gives you enough information to deal with both multiplication and division involving the numbers 5, 10, and other related numbers, too. Some of these are summarized below. For division, follow the same process but in reverse.

TO MULTIPLY BY:	ADD THIS MANY NOUGHTS:	AND DIVIDE BY: (MULTIPLY BY)
5	1	2
10	1	1
20	1	(2)
25	2	4
100	2	1
1000	3	1

Getting to Grips With Fractions

Whether dividing a cake into equal portions, or understanding statistics in a newspaper report, you probably have to deal with fractions every day, although you may not be aware of it. They are easy to cope with as long as you know the logical rules.

Multiplication

Can you remember the rule for multiplying fractions from your schooldays? Even if you can't, the chances are that you know how to do this instinctively. If you had to divide a cake into 2, you would cut it in half; if you had to share that cake between 4 people, you would cut it into quarters. So you obviously know that half of a half is a quarter. Expressed mathematically:

$$\frac{1}{2} \times \frac{1}{2} = \frac{1}{4}$$

This is simply a case of multiplying the numbers above the line (the numerators) together, and the numbers below the line (the denominators) together. This rule applies to any fractions:

$$\frac{2}{3} \times \frac{3}{4} = \frac{6}{12}$$

In this case, for example, 2 out of 3 friends are sharing the remaining three quarters of a cake.

However, the fraction $\frac{6}{12}$ can easily be simplified. When both the numbers above and below the line can be divided exactly by the same whole number, that number can be deleted, or cancelled out. This is because multiplying both parts of the fraction by the same number does not alter the value of the fraction. So:

$$\frac{6}{12} = \frac{6 \times 1}{6 \times 2} = \frac{1}{2}$$

Division

Dividing one fraction by another is made easy by simply knowing one useful trick. Just swap one fraction's components around, and multiply by the other. Say you have 2 cakes, each of a different size. One cake fits $1\frac{1}{2}$ times into $\frac{3}{4}$ of another:

$$\frac{3}{4} \div \frac{1}{2} = \frac{3}{4} \times \frac{2}{1} = \frac{6}{4} = 1\frac{1}{2}$$

Addition and Subtraction

If you want to add 2 fractions, and both have the same number below the line, get your answer by simply adding together the 2 numbers above the line. This is totally logical when you consider that combining the 2 halves of a broken plate makes 1 whole plate. This would be expressed mathematically as:

$$\frac{1}{2} + \frac{1}{2} = \frac{1+1}{2} = 1 \text{ and } \underline{\text{not}} \ \frac{1+1}{2+2} \text{ which equals } \frac{2}{4} \text{ or } \frac{1}{2}$$

As already shown, multiplying both parts of a fraction by the same number does not affect its value. So to make the numbers below the line on both fractions the same, multiply both parts of one fraction by the number below the line, or denominator, of the other. This may sound confusing, but when expressed mathematically, the process should become much clearer:

$$\frac{1}{2}+\frac{3}{4} = \frac{4\times1}{4\times2}+\frac{3\times2}{4\times2}=\frac{4+6}{4\times2}=\frac{10}{8}=1\frac{2}{8}=1\frac{1}{4}$$

Once you have overcome any needless fear of fractions, you can see from the examples above that they can greatly simplify what would otherwise be extremely complex problems if, for example, they were expressed entirely in words.

What's the Point of Percentages?

Fractions can easily be expressed as percentages. A percentage is a proportion of a whole, and that whole is 100 – "per" means "for" and "cent" means 100. We are continually bombarded with percentages: 25% reduction on sale goods; 67% examination pass rate; 8% of a town's population unemployed. Because they sound so important, many people are intimidated by them, but they are really just a way of measuring information so that you can get an accurate picture.

In order to convert a fraction into a percentage, just multiply it by 100. So, if 3/4 of those attending your evening class passed the French exam, you know that:

$$\frac{3}{4} \times 100 = \frac{300}{4}$$

This means that 75% of the students passed, or 3 out of every 4 people. So logically, dividing a percentage by 100 produces the corresponding fraction:

$$75\% = \frac{75}{100} = \frac{3}{4}$$

When calculations involve percentages, it is essential that these are converted into fractions rather than just omitting the percentage symbol. Otherwise, you may get rather more than you bargained for!

Discounts

You will often come across percentages when dealing with special offers on goods. When you want to work out how much you save by buying a washing machine priced at $450 that is reduced in price by 12%, all you have to do is: divide the original price by 100, and then multiply by the percentage in question, or
12 x $4.50 = $54

To find the price you will pay, simply take $54 away from the original price to give $396.

If you just want to find the final price, you can divide the original price by 100, and multiply that by 100, minus the discount offered: **100 – 12 = 88%**
An easy tip to remember every time you have to deal with fractions or percentages is that "of" in this context means "multiply".
So 88% of 200 is

$$\frac{88}{100} \times 200 = 176$$

Price Plus Percentage

To calculate a price that needs to include an additional percentage, for example if you had to add a tax of 20% onto the price of goods, follow this routine:
Calculate the 20% as before, and then add it to the original price. If you have a calculator handy, or you want a bit of a challenge, then the original price can be multiplied by 1 plus the percentage divided by 100.

So, the final cost of a tool costing $80 with a tax of 20% can be written as:

80 x 1.2 = $96

Positive and Negative Numbers

Whenever you sit down to work out the current state of your finances, you are using positive and negative numbers. Any bills you have to pay are negative; your income is positive. Yet the two may easily be confused. Just as the further a positive number is away from nought, the larger it is, the further a negative number is away from nought, the smaller it is: –1000 is smaller than –10.

TEST IT OUT

If you have two bills to pay, one of \$70 and one of \$45, you have a total bill of \$115. So adding 2 negative numbers together still results in a negative number. Expressed mathematically:

(–70) + (–45) = –115 The brackets help to avoid confusion.

But, if you have only one bill of \$70, and have been paid \$100, you clearly have \$30 left over after settling your debts:

(–70) + 100 = 30

In this way, you can begin to see that, if the positive value is greater than the negative, you are left with a positive value, and vice versa.

Now, if \$30 of the bill for \$70 is found to have been a result of overcharging, you must take the \$30 away from the \$70 to find that you only have \$40 to pay:

(–70) – (–30) = (–70) + 30 = –40

Now you can also see how 2 minuses make a plus. Perhaps it is simpler than it first appeared after all!

The Simplest Things in Life

Were you intimidated by the predominantly wordy problems in the self-assessment section? If so, take heart from knowing that a good dose of common sense and logic can be just as helpful as mathematical expertise. Consider the problems below. Would you be able to give an immediate answer?

1. Your boss asks you for a rough evaluation of the results of a survey set up to find out how many teenagers are likely to watch less than 25 hours of television each week. If approximately 30% of those asked were found to spend more than 25 hours a week watching television, and ¾ of a group of 420 teenagers were questioned, what answer would you give your boss?

Don't panic! A rough answer means just that. Try working backward: ¾ of 420 is approximately 300. 30% is roughly ⅓, so about 100 teenagers out of the 300 fall into the more-than-25-hour category. A sensible answer would therefore be:
300 – 100 = 200.

2. You're working to a tight schedule. You've spent just over ⅔ of a 5-day working week on a project, and have got about 15% of it done. You think that the last half, being more complicated, will take double the time. How many weeks do you think it will take to complete the project altogether?

If 15% takes just over ⅔ of a week, then the first 50% equals about 3 lots of this, namely 2 weeks. So the second half takes about 4, and the whole project takes about 6 weeks in total.

Go It Alone

Now build on the hints in the previous pages to try some problems out for yourself.

1. You inherit a share of the fortune of your uncle's cousin once-removed. Three properties, each valued at $155,000 and 4 cars, each worth about 1/3 of each property, together with shares valued at just under $150,000, form the fortune. If you are entitled to 12%, approximately how much is your inheritance worth?

2. You are trying to ascertain roughly how much cash you will have to live on at the end of the month. You are currently $240

in credit, but have a credit card bill of $\frac{2}{5}$ of that to pay at the end of the month, when your salary of $1,250 is paid in. However, you always set 25% of your salary aside to go into your savings account. How much do you reckon on being able to spend?

Answers

1. 27 + (44) = 71 x 3 = (213) – 69 = (144) / (12) = 12 x (7) = 84 – (29) = 55 + (69) = 124.

2. $241

3. A = 14 B = 9 C = 5

Consider each of the 4 larger triangles in turn; each one is subdivided into 4 smaller ones. Multiply the number at the apex of each large triangle by the number in its base triangle, moving in a clockwise direction. Divide the number you get by the number in the next small base triangle to give the number in the small central triangle.

4. C = 5

5. 35 seconds

6.

a) 2.5 (quartered)

b) 202 (x3, +1, or +15, +45, +135.)

c) 8 (halved, +2, or –32, –16, –8.)

d) 95 (–11, –12, –13.)

e) 35 (–9, +10, –11, +12.)

7. 22.

Cats = 4, mice = 7, dogs = 9

8. 297.8 miles

9.

a) 22 x 2 + 22 = 66

b) 44 / 4 + 44 = 55

c) 77 + 77 / 7 = 22

d) 66 + 6 – 6 / 6 = 11

e) 33 x 3 – 33 = 66

10. 3

11. 324

12. One arrow pointing up

13. 48

14. 323

15. 4:30 p.m.

16.

a) 42 (add 21, working upward on each side)

b) 29 (left number + right number = number above left number. Left number + 3 = right number)

c) 26 (right number is worth half of the corresponding left number)

17. $662

18. 7

19. 15

20. 6 (2 birds per cloud; 3 per sun)

21. S = 4, T = 3

22. 1 hour 20 minutes (80 minutes)

Your Score

0-14 Quite poor – but a little work will soon show a rapid improvement.

15-20 Average. You have made a promising start, so keep going!

21-26 Good. You have obviously found the right approach for dealing with numbers.

27-32 Excellent.

Go It Alone

Answers

1. 3 x 150 + 4 x 50 + 150 = 800. Fortune worth about $800,000.

12% = about $\frac{1}{8}$ = about $100,000

2. 2 x 250 = 100. So $150 after credit card. Approximate $1250 to $1200; 75% of which is

5

$900. Left with 900 + 150, about $1050.

Increase Your Creativity

It's a wonderful moment when a sudden insight flashes into your mind, perhaps solving some troublesome problem or conjuring up an ingenious idea. Creative thinking paves the way for a more exciting, less problematic and often more successful life. See how you fare with the creativity self-assessment tests below. Scoring for all these exercises is on pages 82 and 83.

Objective Thinking

Consider the list of objects below. Each has its own particular purpose, but your task is to imagine as many other ways as possible that it could be of some use – the more unusual, the better. For example, a submarine would obviously play its part in naval work, but could also serve as a giant incubating chamber for scientific experiments. Dedicate 5 minutes to each object. Feel free to dismantle, rearrange, fill up, transport to an unexpected environment...

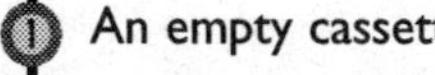

1. An empty cassette case.
2. A filing cabinet.

3. Sydney Opera House.
4. A giraffe.
5. A contact lens.
6. A set of scaffolding.
7. A washing-up liquid container.
8. An electric guitar.
9. The Eiffel Tower.
10. The planet Mars.

Playing with Images

The following phrases conjure up a certain kind of visual image. It's up to you to identify up to 3 equivalent phrases that correspond to each image given. You have 3 minutes to find the most apt and original equivalents for each one.

Example

A balloon let loose in the sky.

Could be conceptually synonymous with:

a. A twig floating on the ocean.
b. A prisoner on being released.
c. A painter facing a blank canvas.

Now try these:

1. Viewing a tennis match from a helicopter above.
2. Losing your voice mid-conversation.
3. A sudden thunderstorm.
4. Climbing a ladder.
5. Hearing a fire alarm.
6. Diving into the sea.
7. A derelict house.
8. Water in a bath draining away.
9. Goldfish in a tank.
10. Leaves of a book flapping in the breeze.

Storytime

If you are happier with words than images, you may find that the following task is a better test of your creative spirit. You are allowed up to 300 words to create a smooth, easily understood narrative. It doesn't matter whether it's fact or fiction, just as long as it makes sense! Seems simple? Well, there's one small additional task you have – as many items as possible from the list below must somehow be woven into the thread of your text. The timing is up to you – this is an opportunity for your imagination to roam freely.

ASSESS YOURSELF

Items to include:

1. A toothbrush.
2. A wild animal.
3. A battle – verbal, physical or otherwise.
4. A long journey.
5. A personal catastrophe.
6. Water.
7. A long telephone call.
8. The acquisition of money.
9. Learning a new skill.
10. An art gallery.
11. A tub of cream.
12. A dictionary.
13. The police.
14. A chance encounter.
15. A candle.

Picture This

Here's another test for the visually creative among you. Study each of the diagrams below for 1 minute, listing as many interpretations as possible of what each one represents.

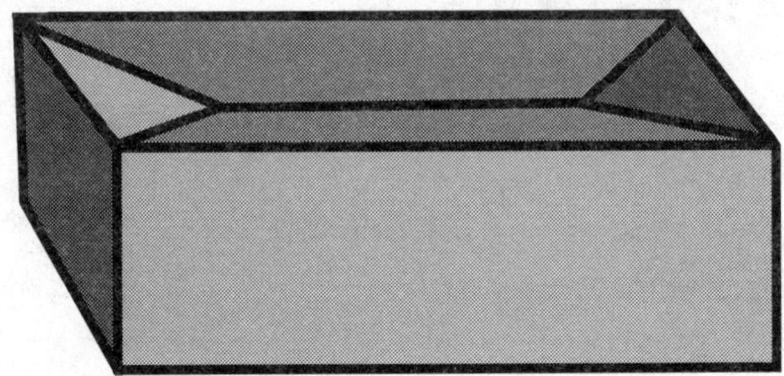

Whether it is interpreted as producing totally new ideas or combining old ideas in a new way, creativity is something that many of us admire and try to acquire. The exact nature and source of creativity seems to be something of a mystery. Its scientific origin has failed to be precisely determined, and many scientists would say that any definite understanding of exactly what it is will always remain a puzzle.

What is It?

Some studies suggest that high levels of creativity are related to the way an otherwise typical nervous system functions, rather than to the structure itself. Perhaps it is because of this uncertainty that a diverse display of creativity continues to flourish. If 'rules' about the precise nature of creativity were to be laid down, this might well stifle all kinds of interesting ideas.

There are, however, various factors that we are fairly certain affect creativity. We know that being able to escape preconceptions, conditioning and convention is a key for fresh thought – who said that the average vehicle has to have four wheels? Past experience and knowledge can help us, and often prevents us from making mistakes, but it can also stop us from trying new paths of thought. The very young are generally less inhibited about changing the rules – because they don't yet know what many of them are.

Early Influences

Childhood plays a vital role in determining our future level of creativity. Everyone is thought to have some creative capacity, so nurturing this skill from an early age can reap huge benefits in later life. The early years can provide a wealth of creative opportunities, and if children are encouraged to explore these actively, rewards are bound to follow later in life. If a parent constantly imposes their view on a child, it will take a very strong-minded child to resist these and forge their own ideas.

Like intelligence, creativity usually lasts into old age – and it may even prolong life. But intelligence is not necessarily related to creativity. Rather than being particularly special, the basic skills that seem to be linked with creativity are actually very ordinary: noticing, recollecting and recognizing. How these are manipulated, however, is where creativity comes in.

Staying Power

Creative success is predominantly the result of sustained effort and motivation rather than any miraculous power – you cannot become a virtuoso jazz pianist overnight! Technical ability plays no less a part than natural talent and significant displays of creativity are unlikely to appear before a decade of dedicated effort. So, child prodigies do not suddenly acquire their ability from nowhere – they simply started before everybody else! This relentless drive often stems from an endless curiosity, an experimental nature, and an overriding desire to break away from the work of predecessors.

Confidence is a vital factor. It takes courage to break away from convention. As we all know, some of the greatest inventions and ideas of our times were considered insane when they were first put forward.

Winging It

Improvising solutions to problems that present no obvious explanation is a sure sign of creative thought. However, this obviously requires a great deal of knowledge and experience – pure creativity stems from learning, but is impossible to learn.

Exactly when, where and how a creative idea is born cannot be scientifically predicted. A sudden flash of insight can come into the mind, seemingly from nowhere, although what has probably happened is that the brain has been working away with the idea subconsciously. The creation of an original idea is therefore ongoing. Your initial confrontation with a problem may appear to be unproductive, but this can have the effect of granting your brain unrestricted freedom to play around with it. From this may come that moment of sudden inspiration, culminating in a rational appraisal of the idea. All that remains to be done is to convince others of your genius!

All of this means that no one, regardless of their abilities, can be relied upon to come up with an appropriate idea at exactly the right moment. Nevertheless, a person's overall creativity is still likely to remain relatively consistent.

Creative Confusion

Creativity can occasionally be confused with ideas that seem original but that actually follow a text-book formula. Editing an existing musical composition, adding bits here and there to make the whole piece appear to be new, is far less creative than composing the piece in the first place. There are countless rules that we all stick to, from how we structure a sentence to how we build a house. Most of us are simply embellishing these when we work, rather than creating the rules themselves.

Whether used to master a particular activity, or merely to cope more efficiently with daily life, an actively creative mind can enhance a range of other mental pursuits. For example, creativity allows much greater abilities of recall. When a topic is approached with an unusual, individual slant, the brain can often access information more quickly. A creative mind is usually a questioning and curious one, in which interest and motivation are kept actively alive and ideas create the desire to discover even more.

Getting Your Point Across

Creativity is all very well, but unless you can persuade others of your talents, it can easily go unnoticed and unappreciated. People might not have the knowledge necessary to understand your ideas, or may be reluctant to accept new ideas. So, it's often not just a question of being creative, but of being able to communicate concepts to those around you.

Testing it Out

If allowed room to breathe, creativity is likely to last a lifetime. A conscious effort to maintain your creativity inevitably leads to a life organized in such a way that your creative performance is maximized. If you face each new problem positively, considering how it could be overcome successfully rather than stating that it is simply impossible to solve, creativity will flow much more easily. But patience is essential – creative ideas need time to hatch and grow; they cannot be expected to appear magically whenever you click your fingers!

The Merits of Motivation

Because you need time and the right opportunities to cultivate your creative spirit, no one can be expected to come up with wonderful ideas on a regular basis throughout his or her lifetime. It will always help if you focus your attention on what you enjoy, rather than what you feel you should be attending to. Try to concentrate on a limited area, rather than casually dipping into a medley of subjects. Devotion to a particular area of interest enables the mind to work through ideas that require considerable time and effort to come to fruition.

Motivation is more likely to thrive if the main force of it comes from you, rather than from outside influences. Being genuinely fascinated by something for its own sake, and not simply because of the rewards it can bring, for example, usually brings a greater depth of creativity. Your surroundings, however, do play an important part. Feeling psychologically safe and free to explore can work wonders. Also, while we shouldn't feel too restricted by other people's demands in order to be truly creative, a little support and praise from others can have a dramatic effect.

The Old and the New

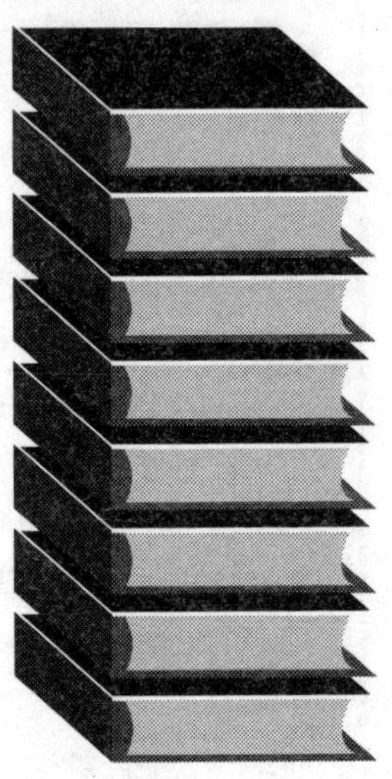

Although you may view creativity as a matter of producing something fresh, give yourself the best possible start by knowing as much as possible about existing ideas before embarking on anything new. A degree of technical knowledge can open your mind up to a wealth of new ideas, sparking off thoughts that may never have occurred to you before. Look at existing information from various perspectives to help you to break away from safe, tried and tested ideas.

Don't let other people's negative reactions automatically interfere with your creative urges. Try to understand and develop your real strengths and talents, and this will give you greater self-confidence. Self-belief and risk-taking form the essence of creative success. Just by looking around you and seeing the range of objects that have originated from someone's creative ingenuity can only serve as an enticement for you to follow suit.

Breaking Away

Approach each creative challenge on your own terms. Try to break away from existing limitations to develop your own interpretation of each task that you face. Too often people restrict themselves by working within a problem rather than reaching out and beyond it. This is illustrated by the exercise below. You may well be familiar with this puzzle, which asks you to join up all the dots with four straight lines without removing your pen from the paper. The solution is on page 152.

Brainstorming

Brainstorming serves as a tremendous aid in improving creativity; decide whether you prefer to do it on your own or with other people. Try simply noting down any thought and association that comes to mind when you focus on a specific task – no matter how bizarre it might seem. You may find that the mere act of writing down the relevant issue in the middle of a blank piece of paper, and creating a web of related ideas branching out from this produces more than enough ideas ready to pursue. Or, if you are working with others, you might simply throw ideas around out loud – perhaps playing word association games and so on. Brainstorming itself needn't be a lengthy process – it is the development of each thought that may take some time.

Whether you are alone or generating ideas with others, relax and let your ideas flow. Speaking continuously, simply saying whatever springs to mind, activates the brain encouraging ideas. Whether your words contain the beginnings of a promising idea, or merely show that no ideas are forthcoming, is irrelevant – take heart from knowing that even the most creative mind lapses every now and again!

In brainstorming sessions, don't:

- stop to worry whether what you are saying is grammatical or beautifully expressed
- feel that you have to justify every thought – in the early stages, simply the fact that you have come up with it yourself makes an idea justifiable; it is only later, after further deliberation, than you need to defend it against possible opposition.

Develop your thoughts as you experience them, as opposed to relating them or writing them down later. Thinking and speaking simultaneously can enable a chain of thoughts to unwind and gradually move toward its full potential. Regardless of whether your chosen instrument is a pen or a paintbrush, music or science, a positive approach and determination help to maximize success. Leave it to others to set the limits and restrictions – telling yourself you can't do it only adds to your obstacles. Don't be your own worst enemy!

Objective Thinking

Your Score

Only you, or preferably an unbiased volunteer, can judge the quality of your responses. However, as a general guide:

0-4 uses for each object: Poor. You probably just need to relax more and your creative ideas will flow more readily.
5-8: Good. You are obviously used to looking at things from all kinds of angles.
Above 8: Excellent.

Playing with Images

Scoring

Award yourself points as follows (or get an obliging friend to help):

0 for failing to respond, or producing an inappropriate, unrelated response.
1 for an appropriate but unoriginal answer (example response: a)
2 points for an appropriate and more original answer (example response: b)
3 points for an appropriate and highly original, imaginative answer (example response: c)

0-40: Poor. Again, you'll find this much easier if you relax and stop looking for the 'right' answer.

41-65: Good. You've got good creative potential but you tend to hold back. Dare to be more adventurous with your ideas!

66-90: Excellent.

Storytime

Scoring

That helpful friend will come in handy again! Starting with a score of 15, deduct one point for the omission of each item. Now award a score out of 5 (5 being the best) for:

a. How well the text flows and general clarity.

b. Degree of interest/amusement/enjoyment derived from your story.

c. Level of original and imaginative thought.

Your Score

0-16: Poor. Your creative muscles just need a bit of exercise.

17-23: Good. Now see how much further you can take your creative ideas.

24-30: Excellent.

Picture This

Your Score.

For each diagram:

0-3 interpretations: Poor.

4-6: Good.

7 or over: Excellent.

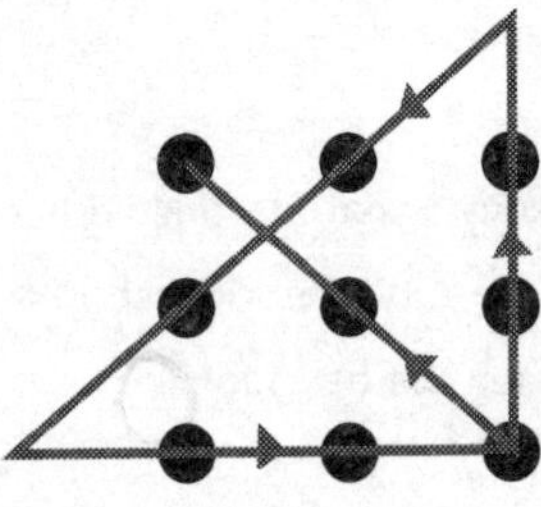

Breaking Away

Most people approach this first by restricting the lines to the square itself; the solution demands that the pen breaks away from the confines of the square. Make sure that, whenever you face a new challenge, you don't always trap yourself within a limiting square.

Making Better Decisions

To be or not to be? To do or not to do? To go or not to go? Every day, a multitude of decisions need to be taken, ranging from which side of the bed to get out of (easier if your bed lies next to the wall!) to deciding to buy a house. Use this self-assessment section to discover which kind of decision-maker you are. Only, however, if you decide that you want to.

Well, I'm Not Too Sure...

Imagine yourself in each of the following situations. Your task is to note which of the reactions you consider yourself most likely to follow. Be honest – you are the only judge.

You drop in to say hello to the person who lives next door. When asked if you would like a drink, do you say:

a. Only if you're making one.

b. I'd love a coffee.

c. Yes, please.

Your roommate says that he feels like cooking a special supper, and asks you what you would like. Do you:

a. Ask what's in the fridge.

b. Say it's up to him.

c. Present him with a specific recipe.

3

You're planning to go abroad with a group of friends for a couple of weeks. When someone asks you where you'd like to go, do you:

a. Say you have no ideas, or just name the first country that comes into your head.
b. Suggest a place visited by a friend or work colleague last year, which they said was very pleasant.
c. Hunt around and look in various brochures before making your suggestions.

4

You and some friends are trying to decide where to go one Saturday evening. Do you decide to:

a. Organize the party, and start ringing venues up to get details about what's on offer.
b. Go along with whatever the others decide.
c. Make a few half-hearted suggestions.

5

After a shopping trip, you discover that the shirt you bought has a hole under the collar. Do you:

a. Take it straight back.

b. Make a mental note to do something about it sometime.

c. Put it down to bad luck and leave it to rot in your wardrobe.

6

You're uncomfortable in your current long-standing relationship and are wondering how to resolve things. Do you:

a. Wait and see what happens.

b. Sit down with your partner to have a serious talk and get things sorted out.

c. Pack your bags and move out.

7

During one evening at home, the noise made by the family next door is driving you crazy. Do you:

a. Spend so long wondering about whether to go round and complain that the noise eventually stops without any interference.
b. Agree with your housemate that it would be a good idea for someone, namely her, to go and complain.
c. Decide to give it another 20 minutes, and if it's still unbearable, go round yourself.

8

A business acquaintance offers you a – more challenging – job out of the blue. Do you:

a. Immediately try to find out more about it.
b. Refuse at once, sticking with your current job for fear of change.
c. Put off making a choice, asking for more time to think it over.

9

Once again, you find yourself struggling with an awkward lock on the front door. Do you:

a. Remind yourself to get a locksmith round next week.

b. Grumble slightly, then forget about it until you next find yourself trying to get into the house.

c. Declare that you can't stand this any more, and get it sorted out immediately.

10

The telephone rings when you're sitting down with your family at home. Do you:

a. Get up and answer it straight away.

b. Ask if you should answer it or is someone else going to?

c. Wait to be asked to answer it.

You open the front door and are greeted by a salesman, who immediately tries to sell you goods you're really not interested in. Do you:

11

a. Tell him you're not interested and shut the door.

b. Say half-heartedly that you're not really sure.

c. End up being persuaded to buy a multitude of things you will never use.

You are asked to do something about a problem that has cropped up at work which requires considerable investigation. Do you:

12

a. Hope that it will improve without undue interference.

b. Start a detailed survey to pinpoint the cause and take the appropriate action.

c. Tackle some of the superficial symptoms ineffectually rather than addressing the root cause.

13

You suspect that the house next door is being broken into after hearing a series of mysterious noises. Do you:

a. Ring for the police straight away.

b. Panic, which is of little help to anyone.

c. Go and tell someone else of your suspicions, leaving it up to them to take any action.

14

You've saved up for a long time to buy a car. The day has finally arrived, but you find yourself torn between two models. Do you:

a. Ask the salesman for his opinion.

b. Toss a coin to decide.

c. Eventually pick one of the models yourself.

15

You're shopping for a pair of shoes to wear to your sister's wedding, and end up finding two pairs that you're really keen on. Do you:

a. Buy both, and decide which pair to wear on the big day.
b. Come home empty-handed, unable to choose which pair to buy.
c. Rationally choose the pair you think you'll get most use out of.

16

Your generous aunt asks you what you would like for your birthday. Do you:

a. Say it's up to her – you can't think of any particular thing.
b. Finally come up with something you know you'll really appreciate.
c. Give her a choice of items off the top of your head.

17

The day of your hairdresser's appointment arrives, and you turn up in the mood for a change of style. In the end, do you:

a. Leave it all up to your hairdresser.

b. Just ask for a trim – again.

c. Describe the different style you want in precise detail.

18

You're not too sure what to do on your longed-for day off. Do you:

a. Set about drawing up a plan of action, and stick to it.

b. Have a marathon couch-potato session.

c. Pass the day without knowing what you've done.

19

An important decision concerning the siting of a new factory is under discussion at work. When asked for your professional opinion, do you:

a. Pick a particular location because it seems a popular choice with everyone else.
b. Compile a list detailing the merits of each site, and make your decision based on this.
c. Select the location closest to your home.

20

During a hectic weekend of apartment-hunting, you've narrowed the options down to three. Do you choose:

a. The place with the nicest view.
b. The apartment without any structural problems.
c. The apartment that comes complete with fitted carpets.

21

You're feeling rather tired and are looking forward to an early night when a friend calls, asking you to go to a party with her. Do you:

a. Explain politely that you've decided to stay in.
b. Ask your friend to call back half an hour later, when you will have made up your mind.
c. Let yourself be persuaded, against your better judgement.

22

You've been invited out on a picnic, but when the day arrives, your fears that the people who are going will not get on well together come to the fore, and you feel reluctant to go. Do you:

a. Go along anyway, attempting to dismiss your fears.
b. Ring up and cancel.
c. Turn up, armed with some games that you could play if the conversation gets really hard-going.

23

A major corporate decision is left to you. You have access to detailed statistical data and surveys of public opinion. Do you make your decision on the basis of:

a. What you can deduce from the available data, despite feeling that your understanding of the statistics is somewhat cloudy.
b. The advice of others, as you don't want to be unpopular.
c. Your own judgement, having sought explanations for anything that you found unclear.

24

A friend telephones you in a state of panic after discovering that her kitchen is flooded. Do you:

a. Try to stop yourself from panicking and rush round at once, forgetting in the rush to take your buckets along.
b. Ask if she's rung for a plumber, offering calming advice before dashing over to give constructive help.
c. Say, 'So what do you think I can do about it?'

25

When completing questionnaires, do you often:

a. Tick the don't know/can't be sure boxes.
b. Respond with a definite yes or no.
c. Ask others nearby what they think.

26

You're going to an auction that promises to offer an intriguing selection of curiosities. Do you:

a. Set yourself a spending limit and stick to it.
b. End up buying a variety of junk despite your good intentions.
c. Return empty-handed – you always seemed to miss your chance.

27

You notice a mysterious clunking noise coming from the engine of your car when you are speeding along the open road on a long journey. Do you:

a. Carry on as before until you reach your destination, hoping it will go away.
b. Slow down a little, listening carefully for a while before turning off somewhere to seek assistance.
c. Nearly cause an accident in your panic to get off the road.

28

You're considering taking an evening class. After browsing through a list of what is on offer, do you:

a. Finally decide on a course that really appeals to you, weighing up the possible future benefits.
b. Feel so overwhelmed by the choice that you put the list aside, but when you do choose you discover it's too late to enrol.
c. Agree to enrol on a course that your friend has urged you to do with him.

29

At work, each member of your department has been asked to compile a report on a different aspect of the company. A list of the various aspects is circulated, from which you are to choose the one that appeals to you. Do you:

a. Claim first pick, having rushed to choose before anyone else has made up their mind.
b. Wait until last, when all except one has been selected.
c. While most options are still up for grabs, consider which topic you know most about.

30

You suddenly realize that you've lost a valuable watch of great sentimental value. Do you:

a. Panic, getting very upset and proceeding to accuse anyone near you of moving/stealing it.
b. Make yourself relax before conducting a meticulous search.
c. Hope that it will turn up later.

Research has so far failed to provide conclusive evidence about the precise areas of the brain responsible for judgement and decision-making – especially intuitive, gut-reaction decision-making. In some 'decisions', the brain is not even consciously involved. For instance, removing a finger that is being burned from a scalding surface happens instantaneously, and is known as a reflex reaction. As well as taking vital unconscious 'decisions' such as this in order for survival, the same sensory pathways in the nervous system are claimed to have some influence over our emotions. Here, the way that we behave is largely dictated by a constant stream of decisions that demand more conscious consideration. These types of decision vary greatly – from what to have for lunch to whether or not to make hundreds of people redundant. The amount of attention that you give to each should obviously be very different.

Taking Responsibility

The making of a decision arises only when the need to do so is recognized in the first place. So, the greater your responsibilities, whether at home or at work, the more dilemmas you will need to resolve. A good decision often requires clarification of a specific objective – deciding to build a new supermarket on a particularly cheap plot of land is futile if public access is limited.

A decision is very rarely thought to be ideal by all the parties involved – what's better for one party may well be detrimental to another. Wise decisions try to ensure that the overall benefits outweigh the costs and come to some sort of thoughtful compromise.

Deciding What to Decide On

How a problem is to be addressed can determine the direction a decision takes. Action can be immediate or delayed, taken either to prevent a certain situation from occurring, or correcting the results later. Acting with an astute mind, anticipating what may happen before it actually does, can relieve much of the pressure of what may otherwise require a far more difficult decision. The best decisions are geared not so much to the perfect outcome as to the best use of the available resources. However well judged the decision, it doesn't mean that a miracle will follow.

Deciding Factors

Obviously, your personality strongly affects your style of decision-making. If you enjoy risk-taking, your decisions will differ dramatically from those made by someone who can never bear to leave anything to chance. So too will your success rate – a determination to be a high-achiever frequently dictates the gambles you decide to take. The same goes for self-confidence. Trusting your instincts and convictions and accepting personal responsibility enables decisions to be taken much faster. Self-doubt is disastrous, as is obstinately sticking to your view without listening to any advice.

You must decide what type of approach is best for the issue in question. The decision-maker who always grabs too quickly at an answer and then spends all their time justifying it might have directed their energies more constructively into reviewing different options in the first place. The logical approach commonly adopted by children can prove highly fruitful: if I did this, then that would happen, which would mean that such-and-such would occur. Unfortunately, such a rational chain of thought is too often considered inferior to more instantaneous decision-making, where the pressures of time render such deliberation unfeasible.

Having said this, intuition certainly has a vital role to play in all kinds of day-to-day decisions. The absence of conscious thought often makes it very difficult to explain exactly what has prompted a particular decision. But just because you cannot fully justify a certain decision does not necessarily mean that it should be dismissed. Technological and scientific advances place more and more emphasis on knowing exactly why you did something, but on an everyday basis, intuitive decisions are invaluable – and have an uncanny tendency to prove themselves right.

Natural Talents

Your natural creativity will strongly influence your approach. If your views are rather narrow and blinkered, you are less likely to make effective decisions. An original, refreshing outlook often produces greater understanding of a problem, allowing the most appropriate decision to be made – if you don't understand all the options available, how can you hope to select the right one?

Another powerful influence is stress, which can have a disastrous effect on the most accomplished decision-maker. The pressures of time, the irritability stemming from fatigue, the draining effects of illness – all can produce poor judgements. The negative feelings that stress produces can also make a bad decision worse by clouding your thinking, making you incapable of taking the right action to try to make things better.

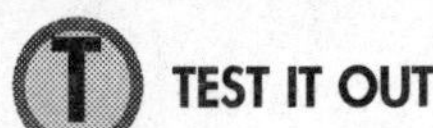

Top Decision-making Tips

1

The need to make a decision often stems from a specific problem. Establishing the root cause of the problem, and that it really does exist, improves your understanding of the situation, enabling the most appropriate action to be taken.

2

Ascertain the importance of your dilemma in order to make a decision of an appropriate scale. Under or over-reacting can have disastrous or simply timewasting consequences.

3

Good decisions usually spring from being fully armed with all the facts. Be suspicious of potentially misleading statistics or biased 'experts'.

4

Although statistical data may be misleading, don't automatically be afraid to use it because of this, or because of a fear of numbers. It can provide valuable insights into a situation, so if you lack the confidence to deal with it, don't be afraid to seek advice from someone who doesn't.

5

Establish exactly what you hope to achieve from each decision you make before making it. Identifying a precise objective helps you to consider appropriate options and seek the best outcome.

6

Avoid being rushed into making a choice whenever possible, especially if you feel that this is impairing your judgement. It can be more beneficial to respond by saying 'can I get back to you?' or 'this isn't a good time' rather than making a hasty decision simply to please someone. Of course, you need to decide whether you are delaying the decision from a conscientious need to consider it further, or just because you are indecisive.

7

If you really are undecided, try jotting down the pros and cons. You may even discover that the grounds for deciding to take action are weak, and that no decision needs to be taken after all!

8

Have the confidence to make bold decisions – don't follow conventional patterns just for the sake of it. When you have to face the consequences of any decision you make, it may as will be one you truly believe in.

9

A fear of questioning other people's decisions can restrict your own decision-making abilities. A creative and original approach to a problem encourages a fresh outlook, providing the means to make wiser, more informed decisions.

It is important to stress the potential rewards of being open-minded, willing to examine the grounds for, and effects of, a decision from all viewpoints. Concentrate on seeking the most acceptable solution for everybody, not simply opting for the easiest choice now, which might prove disastrous in the long-run.

In a business environment, attempting to thrash out every conceivable problem yourself is not advisable. Deciding which decisions to delegate, and to whom, can produce far better results. This makes best use of different people's areas of expertise and means that you can focus your attentions fully on particular decisions, rather than tackling all of them in a rush.

12

Don't be afraid to listen to the opinions of others, but avoid total subordination. People are all too willing to give their advice, but remember that, if it's your decision, you will ultimately have to take the responsibility for it.

13

If you cannot think what options are open to you, let alone pick one, brainstorming may enable you to reach an acceptable solution. This helps avoid unprofitable bouts of panic: 'Help! What am I going to do?'

14

Respect and listen to your intuition.

Do Good Decisions Always Take Time?

Not necessarily. Shrewd, quick-witted thinking can be more effective than hours spent laboriously considering all the options. Only you know what suits you. If you are a spur-of-the-moment, decisive thinker, you are unlikely to gain much benefit from carefully dissecting every option open to you – chances are, you are aware of them already. However, if you feel that your decision-making process is more a matter of continually changing your mind over and over again because of sheer indecision, it's up to you to put a stop to it. Be firm, make that decision, and then stick with it.

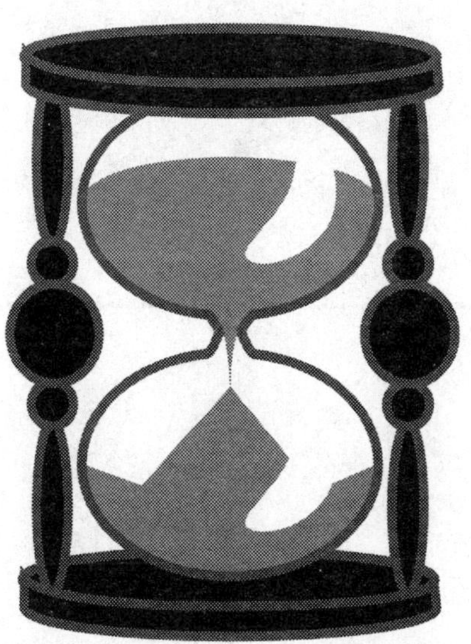

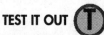

The Good and the Bad

A good decision leaves the situation better than it was before – it's as simple as that. The process you went through may well have been:

- **Identifying the problem, and its cause**
- **Generating various possible options and appraising the relative virtues of each one**
- **Choosing an option and putting it into practice**
- **Monitoring the results.**

Making the Most of a Bad Decision

So, when you come to monitor the results, what can you do if your decision has gone horribly wrong? Don't deny further responsibility or allow it to dent your self-confidence – this could be a potentially enriching opportunity to learn something. It is too easy to view a bad outcome as a lost investment – the investment being time, difficult soul-searching and even a financial loss. Try, if you can, to salvage something from the situation, but if it is a total disaster, don't be afraid to admit that it is, and start again from scratch. Do not stick with something just because you expended a lot of energy on it in the first place; that way, things will go from bad to worse. Take responsibility and do what you can to get things back on the right path.

Self-assessment quiz

Scoring

	a.	b.	c.		a.	b.	c.
1.	0	2	1	**16.**	0	2	1
2.	1	0	2	**17.**	0	1	2
3.	0	1	2	**18.**	2	1	0
4.	2	0	1	**19.**	1	2	0
5.	2	1	0	**20.**	0	2	1
6.	0	2	1	**21.**	2	1	0
7.	0	1	2	**22.**	0	1	2
8.	2	1	0	**23.**	1	0	2
9.	1	0	2	**24.**	1	2	0
10.	2	1	0	**25.**	1	2	0
11.	2	1	0	**26.**	2	1	0
12.	0	2	1	**27.**	0	2	1
13.	2	0	1	**28.**	2	0	1
14.	0	1	2	**29.**	1	0	2
15.	1	0	2	**30.**	0	2	1

Your Score

0-20 You appear reluctant to take decisions, and rely heavily on the judgement of others. Learn to have faith in yourself for once. Be careful not to rush into making a decision just to please someone else; a little more thought now will have much better results later. You could be taking consideration for others too far – sometimes you need to think harder about what you would like.

21-40 You seem to have achieved a good balance between deciding what's best for you and what's best for others. A fear of being wrong may be preventing you from trusting your own instincts more, often preferring to take the safe option rather than going it alone on a matter of some controversy. Take care not to feel pressured – your basic decision-making skills are sound, but may be greatly improved by more thorough exploration of the options open to you. Don't be afraid to ask for advice if you need it.

41-60 You certainly know what you want in life! The assertive confidence you have in yourself helps you to make decisions regardless of what others are pushing you to do. Although you may gain respect for this, watch out for being too self-opinionated, and unwilling to take notice of other people's advice. You are generally able to make a reasoned judgement of a situation, without feeling the need to rush into an inaccurate but prompt decision.

The Art of Communication

Self-assessment

It's impossible to survive without communicating with those around you, whether you're ordering a takeaway or negotiating a crucial business deal. Assess your communication skills by considering the points raised below. Circle the number which you consider to be most appropriate, with 1 representing agreement, 2 sometimes/ can't be sure and 3 disagreement.

1. I often find myself unable to think of something to say to someone. **1 2 3**
2. When I disagree with someone, the conversation normally ends in an argument. **1 2 3**
3. I don't find it very easy to approach a stranger and start a conversation. **1 2 3**
4. Before now, I have felt that people are prejudiced against me because of the image I project. **1 2 3**

5. I tend to avoid making eye contact, particularly when addressing those in a superior position.

1 2 3

6. I have been known to raise my voice and speak slower when trying to make myself understood to people who don't speak my language.

1 2 3

7. I am reluctant to go to parties where I don't know many of the guests as I usually end up standing on my own.

1 2 3

8. I find it difficult to persuade others to agree with my way of thinking.

1 2 3

9. Sometimes, I suspect that whoever I'm talking to is paying little attention to what I'm saying.

1 2 3

10. I tend to cross my legs and fold my arms when sitting down.

1 2 3

11. I'm known more as a talker than a listener.

1 2 3

12. I prefer talking about myself than finding out about other people.

1 2 3

13. If I pass someone I know vaguely in the street, I usually wait for them to say hello.

1 2 3

14. People can take me or leave me – I'm not prepared to change myself for anyone.

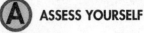

1 2 3

15. I'm really quite shy, although strangers tend to mistake this for sullenness.

1 2 3

16. I have an unfortunate tendency to say the wrong thing at the wrong time.

1 2 3

17. I prefer to launch straight into a debate, rather than planning what I want to say first.

1 2 3

18. I have come unstuck in job interviews before now, rambling on and on, not knowing what I am saying or when to stop.

1 2 3

19. I feel uneasy in unfamiliar social situations, and have no idea what to say.

1 2 3

20. I have been known to upset people unintentionally when what I say doesn't come out quite as I meant it to.

1 2 3

21. I don't like using the telephone as I feel pressured into talking, often unable to get my point across properly.

1 2 3

22. I'm not normally the one who is nominated to be spokesperson when something important needs to be said.

1 2 3

23. If I've delegated a task to someone else, it tends not to be carried out exactly as I would like, because my instructions aren't very clear.

1 2 3

24. I usually grab whatever clothes are at hand, rather than carefully considering what would be most appropriate.

1 2 3

25. I have quite a small, select circle of friends, as people don't approach me very often.

1 2 3

26. I can become so involved in talking about myself that I forget that anyone else is there.

1 2 3

27. I always say precisely what I think, regardless of who I'm talking to.

1 2 3

28. I can talk to someone for hours, then come away without knowing anything about them.

1 2 3

29. I much prefer to let other people do the talking.

1 2 3

30. Sometimes I upset people, not quite realizing how or why.

1 2 3

Would You… or Wouldn't You?

Now consider each of the situations described below, selecting the action you (honestly!) consider yourself most likely to take.

You've been working on a somewhat controversial idea which you hope will earn you a pay rise as it's aimed at increasing your company's turnover. When you next speak to your boss, do you:

a. Launch into explaining your idea confidently, saying how inefficient you think the company is at present.

b. Request a convenient time to propose your idea, outlining its possible future benefits.

c. Fail to mention it at all, as you doubt that the boss will listen to you anyway.

2

You suddenly find that you are the only one talking in a room full of people. Is this most likely to be because:

a. Your words and generally appealing manner have captured everybody's attention.
b. You are so absorbed by what you are saying that you have failed to notice the call for silence.
c. Everyone else has fallen asleep.

3

At a party, you notice a stranger who you would like to start talking to. To attract his or her attention, do you:

a. Ask the host to introduce you, feeling too shy to wander over yourself.
b. Walk over confidently and start elaborating on your life history.
c. Carefully make eye contact, waiting for a positive response before initiating a conversation.

The day of an important business interview arrives. When you get ready, do you:

a. Put on the clothes you selected last night, neatly pressed and hung up, ready for action.
b. Reach for the suit you find buried in the back of your wardrobe, only to discover you have no time left to replace the missing button.
c. Throw anything on, as long as it's clean.

You discover that the television you have just purchased is faulty. Do you:

a. Take it back to the retailer, or phone them, explaining your problem and politely request a prompt repair or exchange.
b. Ask a friend if they will approach the retailer as you don't get very far when complaining.
c. End up being fobbed off by the retailer and putting up with the faulty TV.

6

You are trying to convert an acquaintance to your way of thinking during a heated debate. When you reach the end of the discussion, is it most likely that:

a. Your acquaintance has stormed off in a huff, after you insulted her for her beliefs.

b. You both recognize that the other has a valid point, but agree to differ.

c. Your acquaintance has relinquished her argument, finally agreeing with yours.

A mock trial during a business training weekend requires you to defend the accused despite your underlying conviction of his guilt. Do you:

a. Present a weak case, convincing the jury more of your incompetence than the innocence of the accused.

b. Argue the case with courage and conviction, seizing solely on the evidence that backs up your position.

c. Have a good stab at it, but end up presenting a confused and unduly complicated argument.

8

Which do you consider to be of most importance when first attempting to impress a potential employer?

a. Being well read.
b. An appropriately smart appearance.
c. How many impressive people you know.

9

You're trying to convince an audience of the validity of your argument during a public speech. To help achieve your aim, do you end up:

a. Following a rational line of thought, gradually building up the evidence for your point of view in order to minimize any disagreements.
b. Delivering a carefully rehearsed speech, but coming unstuck and confused when questioned.
c. Speaking louder and louder, in the hope that your confidence and sheer volume will disguise the weaknesses of your argument.

You wish to approach your rather daunting boss to ask for a well-deserved raise. Do you:

a. Chatter on about why you should get a raise without letting your boss get a word in.
b. Bluntly deliver your request, presenting an ultimatum that backfires against you.
c. Politely reason with your boss, explaining your justification to your advantage.

You're trying to negotiate the price and conditions for which a reputable electrician will rewire your house. Do you:

a. Flatly declare that you consider the estimate to be unreasonable, informing the electrician that she can take it or leave it – she leaves it.
b. Reach a compromise whereby both you and the electrician come to an amicable agreement.
c. Allow yourself to be manipulated by the electrician, agreeing without too much resistance to pay a higher price than you would like to.

Plans to build a huge supermarket that would severely disrupt life near your home are put forward. You greet them with strong opposition. Do you voice your concerns by:

a. Writing a persuasive letter to a local political figure, attached to a weighty petition that you have organized.

b. Ruthlessly hunt down the proposers of the plan, hysterically threatening them with the future action you are prepared to take.

c. Sell up before the construction team starts to arrive.

During the course of your professional duties, you find yourself having to make several employees redundant. Do you:

a. Shirk responsibility, attempting to nominate someone else to tell them – you'll only say it all wrong.

b. Flatly inform the workers of their misfortune, preferring to stick to the facts to avoid getting too personally involved.

c. Deliver the news as kindly as possible, offering what few words of comfort you can.

One of your housemates has an annoying but unnecessary habit that is seriously frustrating you. Do you:

14

a. Drop unsubtle hints until your grievance has been noted.
b. Explain directly to your housemate that you don't want to start an argument, but...
c. Start plaguing your housemate with an equally annoying habit of your own.

You've felt yourself drifting away from your partner for some time, but have been reluctant to admit it. When your partner broaches the subject and asks exactly what's wrong, do you:

15

a. Say nothing's wrong – you've just been feeling a bit down lately.
b. Vent your frustration, so you end up having a massive row that achieves nothing.
c. Awkwardly explain that you think you need to talk, trying to couch your feelings in the clearest, kindest manner.

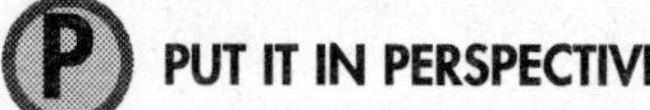

This is the age of advanced technological communication, but what about relating to people on a personal level? It seems that we all have some way to go where this skill is concerned. Whether causing major corporate problems, or needlessly provoking a petty argument, communication problems are all around us. The difficulties are intensified when cultural and social differences come to the fore.

The complexity inherent in even the most basic conversation – where a grammatically clear and logical word sequence must be formed, delivered, understood and appropriately responded to within a pretty brief timespan – is rarely considered. And it is not just words that must be taken into account. Gestures, facial expression, body language, tone of voice – and even clothes and hairstyle – are all-important, and when they contradict whatever is being said this can cause enormous confusion. We all know that stressing one word rather than another can alter the message we are putting across.

Tools of the Trade

The fact that there are so many tools at your disposal when you are relating to others makes communication an exciting, varied experience. The vocal chords and mouth can produce a huge range of sounds, complemented by all kinds of facial movements and expressions: dilation of the pupils, blushing, smiling, crying...

Your eyes say a great deal about you, from silently expressing a welcome to revealing a guilty secret. Conversation benefits greatly from frequent eye contact, whether demonstrating interest, enforcing opinions, or indicating the need for a response. But a careful balance is vital to ensure the comfort of all parties. When eye contact is non-existent, people may think that you really find inspecting your fingernails much more interesting than talking to them. But people will recoil with discomfort if you fix them eyeball to eyeball throughout an entire conversation.

The messages your clothes send out are easier to control, which is fortunate because they can have a very powerful impact, revealing all kinds of things about your attitudes and lifestyle. Your clothes and self-presentation can also reveal a great deal about your creative side, long before you've had a chance to say anything about your ideas. Success in life frequently stems from an ability to tailor this stream of verbal and non-verbal messages to a particular environment.

A Key to Success

Considering how easily an ordinary conversation between two people can falter, when this is magnified, for example, within a large company, the results can be disastrous. Failure to inform certain departments in a company of whatever is going on could prevent adequate general discussion of a business' problems, so a single communication problem can gather a catastrophic momentum. Used positively, to build bridges toward others, the rewards of effective communication will be great and it can certainly be a key to business success. Consider the amount of job specifications asking for a 'good telephone manner' or 'excellent interpersonal skills.'

Assert Yourself

All of us would benefit from communicating more assertively – stating what we want clearly and listening carefully to what others want. Assertive does not mean domineering. It is merely a way of letting people know where they stand and allowing everyone to get what they want from a situation – in other words, good communication.

Establishing an initial rapport with people is vital for easy, enjoyable conversation. Judge your greeting carefully. Although some countries are renowned for their very physical greetings, embracing a stranger in the middle of the street is unlikely to communicate a good impression anywhere in the world.

At Ease!

Early signs of warmth and friendliness encourage all parties to feel instantly at ease. This emotional comfort fosters trust, which in turn brings much smoother discourse. Minimizing disruptions gives each speaker more of a chance – don't keep asking someone if they want more coffee when they are in mid-sentence! Introducing an amusing note is always a good way to dissolve tensions, but be careful to strike the right tone – the amusing tales you tell your closest friends may not be appreciated by your bank manager. Conversely, try to avoid being so quiet that you are thought to be hostile or aloof. Remember, even if you can't think of anything to say, smiling and making encouraging noises always helps, and you may find that this helps your shyness to ebb away naturally as you ease yourself gently into the conversation.

What Now?

As the conversation progresses, take into account the following points:

Be aware of how you are judging people – and how they are judging you. Signals of disapproval that you may send out unconsciously may instigate a row. Dressing to suit the situation may also bring rewards.

2

Adapting your language and manner, as well as your clothes, to the person you are dealing with is considerate and establishes a good understanding between you. If you get it wrong, you can build an immediate barrier that is very difficult to break down. This isn't to say that your conduct should constantly mirror that of others around you - just be aware of how you can get along with others more sensitively.

3

What you don't say can be as important as what you do. Attentive listening, questioning others rather than talking continually about yourself, is always appreciated. By concentrating closely on what is being said to you, you can find yourself in a better position to respond in the most effective manner. Remember that people naturally enjoy talking about themselves – a willingness to listen will win you many friends.

4

Consider other people's reactions to you in order to assess how well you are communicating. If all you are met with is a yawn (or even a snore!), the chances are your words are not exciting much interest. But don't just notice it and feel discouraged or angry – act on the feedback you receive.

5

As to the feedback you give out, use it to your advantage. Communicate your interest by smiling, nodding, making eye contact and using positive words of encouragement. Crossing your arms and legs creates a body-language barrier; it is a defensive position indicative of unease and a reluctance to listen. Open yourself up to others and they will respond in kind.

6

To help gain and sustain people's attention, vary the pitch and tone of your voice. A dull and monotonous monologue, lacking any variety of expression, does little to win people over. Also, don't bombard people with an endless stream of words. Momentary pauses, attending to minor interruptions from others, and supporting your argument with gestures, are all-important when striving to become a successful communicator.

If arguing a particular point, little is gained by adapting a louder, more aggressive voice. This often simply alienates you from others. A raised voice indicates anger and a desire to dominate, inevitably leading to anger on the other side too. A gently persuasive, coherent argument is more likely to produce the result you desire.

8

Maintaining clarity is essential for communicative success. Think clearly before speaking so that you are easily understood. A succinct argument can be more powerful than a rambling, illogical lecture. Good articulation and an air of certainty are greatly beneficial. If you don't know what you mean, how can you expect anyone else to? Devising a plan outlining what you want to communicate to someone during an important conversation could be useful, while simultaneously boosting your confidence.

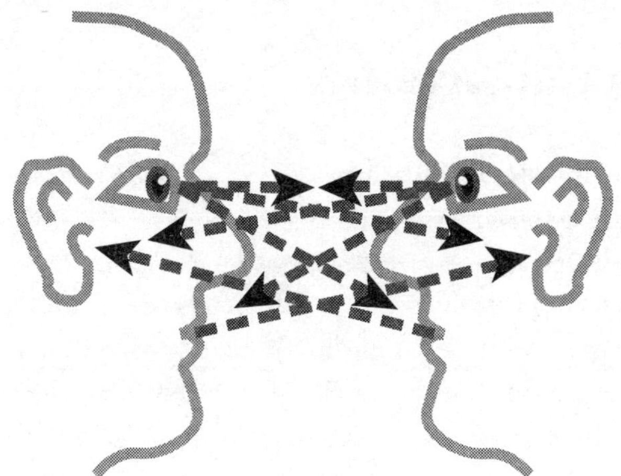

Negotiating Skills

Successful negotiation involves establishing a degree of persuasive, not overbearing, influence. A good rapport provides a better foundation on which to construct a framework for negotiation. During the discussion, act assertively but avoid aggression. Restrain any desire to score points by shouting, making unpleasant or sarcastic remarks or trying to appear superior. Attempts to appease and reason with your listener will nearly always be more productive. Your confident manner can be enhanced by friendly gestures. This attracts more respect and co-operation than a fiercely dominant approach. As always, regular eye contact enforces your viewpoint and expresses your confidence and determination. It is important to physically demonstrate your interest and assertion, while taking care not to emit an overwhelming stubborness.

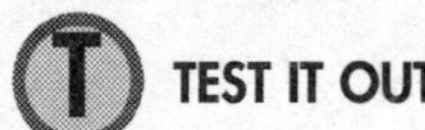

Plan of Action

You are unlikely to meet with much success if you launch into negotiation without thinking about what you hope to achieve. The plan outlined below aims to prevent this.

1

ESTABLISH the situation in your own mind – what you have to bargain with; how far you're willing to compromise; any result you would find unacceptable. Ensure that you know the facts.

2

DISCUSS the situation with the relevant party, each of you clarifying how you view the situation and voicing your respective needs.

3

PROPOSE a solution, generally involving a degree of compromise. Be open to suggestions – you may reach a compromise you hadn't envisaged but that satisfies you more than your original plan.

4

CONCLUDE the negotiation properly, having established what terms both parties have come to an agreement about. Be amicable – it doesn't take much to please others, and can reward you immensely in a tight corner.

Remember: anything is possible if you want it that much.

Deciding what you want is half the battle – then all you have to do is do it!

General self-assessment quiz

Your Score

20-33 Good communication isn't really one of your strongest points. You may find it easy to talk to others, but have you really considered if your words of wisdom are appreciated? Continually focusing on yourself is unlikely to make a good impression. Or perhaps you find it hard to say anything at all, which can be just as bad: people may interpret this is as unfriendliness, rather than shyness. Relax, concentrate on being interested in others rather than worrying about yourself, and things will improve. You should try to be more willing to adapt to each situation: for example, you may create a more favourable impression by considering the dress, attitudes and conversation that fit a particular occasion.

34-47 Although you seem to make quite an effort where communication is concerned, you are prone to lapses that let you down. These may easily be corrected by a more thoughtful, considered approach – clarifying exactly what you want to get out of each situation may provide sufficient insight to help you achieve the results you deserve. Lack of confidence may be all that is holding back your communication skills.

48-60 Your shrewd ability to act according to the situation, gauging how to conduct yourself most appropriately, is very admirable. You appear to be aware of others, recognizing the need to listen in order to put your own thoughts across with the maximum effect. Your popularity stems from your willingness to approach others and be approached – you know that a friendly smile or gesture is just as effective as saying hello. Don't get complacent though – there are always new communication skills to learn.

Would You or Wouldn't You?

Scoring

	a.	b.	c.		a.	b.	c.
1.	1	2	0	**9.**	2	1	0
2.	2	0	1	**10.**	1	0	2
3.	1	0	2	**11.**	0	2	1
4.	2	1	0	**12.**	2	1	0
5.	2	0	1	**13.**	0	1	2
6.	0	1	2	**14.**	1	2	0
7.	0	2	1	**15.**	0	1	2
8.	1	2	0				

Your Score

0-10: Poor. But everyone can learn to communicate better.

11-20: Good, although acting with a little more sensitivity and confidence may be worthwhile.

21-30: Excellent. You seem to be sensitive to the unique communication skills required for each situation.

Improve Your Concentration

- When you are reading, do you ever finish a page and then feel as though you've instantly forgotten what you've just read?
- Have you been present during a conversation where someone has asked you a question but all you are vaguely aware of is that your name has been mentioned – you have no idea what you've been asked?
- Have you ever had a near miss while driving because you simply didn't see the other person coming?
- Do you ever get restless or spend a long time procrastinating when you are given a specific task to do?
- Has anyone sat you down and explained exactly how to carry out a task, and yet soon afterward you can't remember where to begin?

If you answered "yes" to any of the above – then you are in the majority! Lack of concentration is a problem at one time or another for most people. It is also highly infuriating, whether you are the one whose attention has wandered, or you are trying to get through to someone who is not following a word that you're saying. Have a go at the following problems, which have been designed to test your ability to concentrate, and then read on to discover how you can develop this vital skill. Solutions to the tests and exercises in this colour section are to be found on page 223.

Find the Letter Pairs

Read through the following table at a steady pace, counting the number of pairs of letters that are one letter away from each other in the alphabet. For example, one such pair would be AC. Only count pairs found when the alphabet is read from A to Z (so, CA is ignored).

1. AFEMOXZNLQHPWHJAMKVESPRT
   GHOPQSTVCAPLHJXSWYWXLHIOA

2. NPUDEIUZVXPUKPRUFJNBADGUO
   SUXASBTCGWIJLUPMHDADADWP

1. AFEMOXZNLQHPWHJAMKVESPRTG HOPQSTVCAPLHJXSWYWXLHIOA

2. NPUDEIUZVXPUKPRUFJNBADGUO SUXASBTCGWIJLUPMHDADADWP

3. LOSVADHKNPWGURUSJKNORTVD GOIWPURJGBMDOKEKUKIKSYBE

4. UYBFNLBDOQWZJOHCACWYMHC QVXHMOVXHTAOUIGIVBVIPXCHOT

5. FHORVZAFCDMNHJWYOQGOZXZ DRAHJUMIEBYFHVMOBIJKWZADIO

6. CBAIKWOWOWOQZVHJCLOWIOXA FMTVXWVYVWVXZHBFOUYEINUYZ

7. TVADGJMPSVYZARNPHEFTXMLJB ETYHOMJDISYMEARYGPBJYZA

8. HCERWFKLKLKMUBIJCVZBHPVEK OXZFHJUGBOVZYBKPRCMFOHQD

9. HCEADBCECABDCGLBTYMHDLNV ZHEAMUZFBTYGIVSJHCKMVYZIB

10. MDMPYFBHOVZAHMSUWKCUYIHC
VZEMNOPEGKJXNDAEOEULGCVBK

11. EGPQRTVEANRWZDLTYKRZAHOP
DFHIJKDUVOIZXJEHJPKCRSUAC

12. BCUOHMERPRFKTZBHOVZIHCESG
HCDEOWZEMOVHBLRZEJWIADVY

13. GBOPHCMWZHCPRFBMVZHUCLM
OHVNIEARVXACENGYALDRYCLYER

14. JLMNRSTYZDCMNFGCZFMROGLZ
CIPUWIJLEGVCMTYIDOPWFBRYD

15. CIRTYADIMOYHCVRHBTGVZCLMO
YHBRYZTVFOWYHCAKOXPFBLAM

16. ACEUQFMXIPRBIJDFZHCSWGMO
EGBIOVJDANUZAISYICWKEGZBL

17. ZXHARTYAUETRGIZNFCQVYDLUW
CAFCLOWZGBRVYXZVWMLHCHLB

18. YGBMTYEKOGIPRZIDAMSYENVZI
DPWYKDAJWPIDACVJDWMFBVZG

19. JCRWEGYVZJDARZHBDWKFARYF
AZJEDBDZKEBTZJEOWZFBRYNPA

20. ICENPOMFAGBWEKCMVJLDEFGVW
FHWSUAMGWHJLEOYVFHCRAOHC

21. HBIWNFRTHCTHYFLWYDKOFMAR
YFIKEBVYHDYIEACHMHCULYZQR

22. BIOWDMEFVKFNYAZHBPFWZENHB
UFQYGAOFVDAMNQVHCWZCPGYA

23. OFBOVXDAOFRTGHIKYDZBDPGW
HAYEOFYMOGBDYMICIVYDACKEN

24. MEUCJAIVGIPEMCORTFLCJLCSBD
YMIAOJCEERHAWFHYEOHBWFQ

25. ACIWEPGIWCNEVIVTVGHTIBGYM
ESHAPRDUEWBYFHEUGAYDTBLF

Following a Narrative

This passage, from Jane Austen's 18th-century novel *Pride and Prejudice*, contains a number of deliberate errors. Your task is to find out how many. Read the passage through just once, but at a comfortable pace. When concentration is really vital, for example, when you are on the road, you don't get a second chance.

My deer Miss Elizabeth, I hve the highess opinionon in thee world of your' excelllent judgement in n all mattars within the scope off your undererstanding,, but permit me to say that their must be a wide differance betweeen the establiished forms ot ceremony amongst the layity, and those which regulate the clergy;: four give me leave to observe that I consider the clerical offfice as equal in in point of dignitie with the highest rank in tha kingdom – proovided that a proper humility of behavour is at the same time maintaineded. You must therfore alllow me to follow the dictates of my concsience on this ocassion, which leads me too perform what I look on as an point of duty; Pardon me by neglecting to profit buy you're advice, which on evry other subject shall be my constant guide, though in the case before us I consider myself more fitted by educcation and habitual studie to decide on what is right then a young lady like yourself..”” And with a low bow he left him to attack Mr.. Darcy, whose reception of

ASSESS YOURSELF

his advances she eagerly watched, and whose astonnishment at being so addresed was very evident.) Her cousin prefaced his speach with a solemm bow, and 'though she could not here a word of it, she felt as if hearing it all, and saw in th motion of his lips the words 'apology', 'Hunsford', and 'Lady Catherine de Bourgh. – It vexed her to see him expose himsef to such a woman. Mr. Darcy was eyeiing him with unrestrained wander, and when at last Mr. Collins allowed him time to speak, replied with a air of distant civililty. Mr.Collins, however, was not discouraged from speaking again, and Mr. Darcy's contemt seemed abundently increasing with the lenght of his seconds peech, and at th end of it he only made a slight bow, and moved another way Mr Colins then returned to Elizabeth.

How did you do? Within the block above, there are 60 errors of modern grammar. Finding 50+ is excellent; less than 25 is poor. By line, the errors are 1 - 3 (deer, hve, highess), 2 - 4 (opinionon, thee, your', excelllent), 3 - 2 (n, mattars), 4 - 4 off, undererstanding, „ , their), 5 - 3 (diffarance, betweeen, establiished), 6 - 2 (ot, layity), 7 - 3 (;:, four, give), 8 - 3 (offfice, in in, dignitie), 9 - 2 (tha, proovided), 10 - 1 (maintaineded), 11 - 2 (alllow, concsience), 13 - 5 (an, ;,   me, by, buy), 14 - 2 (you're, evry), 15 - 0, 16 - 2 (educcation, studie), 17 - 1 ("""), 18 - 1 (Mr..), 19 - 1 (astonnishment), 20 - 1 ()), 21 - 2 (speach, 'though), 22 - 2 (here, th), 23 - 0, 24 - 1 (.–), 25 - 2 (sef, eyeiing), 26 - 1 (wander), 27 - 1 (Mr.Collins), 28 - 0, 29 - 2 (contemt, adundently), 30 - 3 (lenght, seconds peach, th), 31 - 1 (way , Mr), and 32 - 0.

The nature of concentration differs slightly from the other skills examined in this book. Fairly basic literacy and numeracy skills can be enough to get you through life – but the slightest lapse in concentration may have serious consequences, depending on circumstances. For example, many a road accident is the result of a distracted driver forgetting that he or she was driving – most drivers have experienced the distressing feeling of arriving at a destination without realizing quite how they got there. Inefficient concentration when out shopping might merely mean taking another trip to buy that forgotten loaf of bread, but an air traffic controller's low levels of concentration could be responsible for a major disaster.

Making New Connections

While poor concentration when studying a particular subject is not life-threatening, it can prevent you from grasping the real depth and nature of that subject properly. To see beyond the surface of any information and get the very most from it requires sustained concentration. In many cases, this means that, instead of just taking in an isolated fragment of information that is of little use on its own, the brain links up new learning to existing chains of thought. In this way, knowledge is built upon more rapidly because learning and recall processes work much more efficiently. If you have a poor memory, it is unlikely that this is because you constantly forget information – an initial lack of concentration has probably stopped it from being absorbed in the first place. You can't remember what you don't know!

A Little at a Time

Even the most extraordinary powers of concentration cannot enable us to keep all kinds of demanding knowledge consciously in our minds at the same time – good concentration involves total absorption. It is impossible to keep track of a movie plot while holding an intelligent conversation, reading a newspaper article and learning how to use your new lawnmower!

You will never progress well with your learning if you try to tackle too much at any one time, especially if the information relates to several different subjects. This limits the mind's ability to undertake the kind of probing that is necessary to understand things completely.

With the constant barrage of information going on around us, the brain often has to 'choose' which message to listen to. We are often not even aware that this is happening, because it may take place on a subconscious level. Most of us must have found it quite easy to concentrate on a television programme, while remaining completely oblivious of a conversation going on nearby. However, once you become conscious that this is what you are doing, it becomes much more difficult to block out that conversation.

It has been suggested that there is one central unit within the brain that controls information processing. It seems that the rate of processing is increased if the rest of the brain acts as a kind of filter for this central unit, restricting concentration to a single sensory path. So, although the mind has chosen to focus on the television programme, the nearby conversation may subconsciously be heard, but not attended to. It is still possible to maintain some knowledge of the conversation, although this may be limited to a few seconds of short-term memory. Your decision about what to concentrate on determines which path of information is dealt with properly by the brain – you may well, by chance, remember snippets of a conversation overheard while you were concentrating on watching the television, but relying on being able to recall them would be unwise!

Concentration – an Absorbing subject

It is said that:

The most that someone's attention can alternate between tasks is twice a second.

The maximum time for which we can concentrate on one subject is considered to be just 4 seconds.

Effective concentration involves total absorption. Your degree of concentration is largely determined by you, and not simply by the distractions that you encounter.

The working of circuitry in the brain has been blamed for our reduced ability to concentrate on several tasks at once. If you are already focusing on a subject by using the path of one particular brain circuit, attempts to use the same path to carry out another task may break your concentration on the former. However, if you do need to focus on more than one subject, you can help yourself greatly by making full use of all of your senses.

Don't be too eager to criticize your powers of concentration. You are bound to have experienced moments where your attention has been completely transfixed, perhaps by a stunning sunset or a haunting piece of music. So you know that you have the ability to concentrate completely. Unfortunately, everyone's concentration is constantly being broken by an endless stream of distractions. Learn to deal with these properly and you will soon see a huge difference.

Diminishing Distractions

There are a few golden rules when it comes to dealing with distractions:

Acknowledging a distraction enables you to take control and deal with it. Simply realizing that you are being distracted helps you to focus your attention in the right direction.

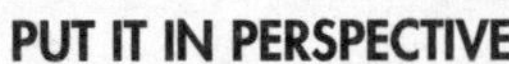

Try monitoring your performance by assessing your levels of concentration. Ask yourself: is your mind in focus or is it liable to wander? Are you really absorbing the information you are studying or merely skimming the surface? It's all too easy to read words without understanding what they mean. This not only wastes time, but denies you the benefits that concentrated reading will deliver.

Ensure that you are fully aware of exactly what the task in question is. Identifying your purpose focuses and maintains your attention and reduces mental distractions.

Stick with one subject at a time in order to direct your attention properly. Physical distractions are as dangerous as mental ones, but are removed with far less effort.

Ensure that any work area remains uncluttered and free from potential distractions.

If you are working at home, set aside a specific area for the task in hand – this also means that you are continually reminded of your purpose.

If your profession is home-based, you may find that dressing as if you were going out to work produces a more focused mind, better able to resist any temptation to wash the bath/dog/car – the kind of tasks that suddenly become irresistibly interesting when trying to concentrate on work. The telephone can prove to be a deadly destroyer of concentration – an answerphone could be an indispensable concentration aid, provided you are not tempted to check it after every call!

SOLUTIONS

Find the Letter Pairs

Total of 131 pairs.

Line break-down: 9, 5, 4, 7, 8, 7, 2, 6, 6, 3, 8, 3, 5, 4, 5, 7, 4, 4, 4, 8, 4, 0, 7, 6, 5.

Your Score

99 or less: Poor.

100-114 : Good.

115-130: Excellent.

IF YOU'VE ENJOYED THIS BOOK, WHY NOT TRY THE OTHERS IN THIS MENSA SERIES:

Title	ISBN	Author	Price
Mensa Boost Your IQ	1 85868 308 4	Carolyn Skitt & Harold Gale	£4.99
Mensa Number Puzzles	1 85868 309 2	Harold Gale	£4.99
Mensa Riddles & Conundrums	1 85868 310 6	Robert Allen	£4.99
Mensa Word Puzzles	1 85868 311 4	Harold Gale	£4.99
Mensa Number Puzzles For Kids	1 85868 312 2	Carolyn Skitt & Harold Gale	£3.99
Mensa Mind Mazes For Kids	1 85868 313 0	Robert Allen	£3.99
Mensa Word Puzzles For Kids	1 85868 314 9	Robert Allen	£3.99
Mensa Secret Codes For Kids	1 85868 315 7	Robert Allen	£3.99
Mensa Logic Brainteasers	1 85868 545 1	Philip Carter & Ken Russell	£4.99
Mensa Mind Workout	1 85868 546 X	Josephine Fulton & Robert Allen	£4.99
Mensa Know Yourself	1 85868 547 8	Josephine Fulton	£4.99
Mensa Visual Brainteasers	1 85868 548 6	John Bremner	£4.99

These Mensa books and many others are available from all good bookshops, or they may be ordered by telephone from Books By Post on (01624) 675 137.